Hallowed *be thy* Name

Living by the word of God

JIM McMANUS C.Ss.R.

A Redemptorist Publication

Published by **Redemptorist Publications**
A Registered Charity limited by guarantee. Registered in England 3261721.

Copyright © Jim McManus C.Ss.R., 2009

First published in 1996 by Darton, Longman & Todd Ltd.
This revised edition in November 2009 by Redemptorist Publications.

Layout by Rosemarie Pink
Cover illustration copyright © Andrew Bezear

ISBN 978-0-85231-365-7

All rights reserved. No part of this publication may be reproduced, stored in a retrieval system, or transmitted in any form or by any means, electronic, mechanical, photocopying, recording or otherwise, without prior permission in writing from Redemptorist Publications.

The moral right of Jim McManus to be identified as the author of this work has been asserted in accordance with the Copyright, Designs and Patents Act 1988.

The names of some people and places have been changed.

A CIP catalogue record for this book is available from the British Library

Printed by Stanley L Hunt (Printers) Limited, Northamptonshire, NN10 9UA

Redemptorist
PUBLICATIONS
Alphonsus House Chawton Hampshire GU34 3HQ
Telephone 01420 88222 Fax 01420 88805
rp@rpbooks.co.uk www.rpbooks.co.uk

Contents

In memory of my sister Celia and my brother Thomas,
who died while I was preparing this new edition.

Introduction

When I published the first edition of this book in 1996 I hadn't fully realised that we were at the beginning of what has been called "the spirituality revolution".[1] It is surely a divine irony that as the Western industrialised world has become evermore determined to keep God and religion out of the public forum, a pang of spiritual hunger is being experienced at the heart of the most secularised societies.

As religion is being pushed to the margins through secularisation, spirituality and the awareness that there is a spiritual dimension to human life are progressively moving centre stage. This revolution is taking place in the midst of people who may never have had any kind of religious affiliation. The sociologist of religion Grace Davie makes the helpful distinction between believing and belonging. The vast majority of people in Britain *believe* in God but they don't *belong* to Church or Synagogue, Mosque or Temple.[2] And within Europe, where secularism as an anti-religious movement was born,

---

1 David Tacey, *The Spirituality Revolution: The emergence of contemporary spirituality* (Hove: Brunner-Routledge, 2004). See also Jeremy Carrette and Richard King, *Selling Spirituality: The silent takeover of religion* (London: Routledge, 2005).

2 Grace Davie, *Europe: The Exceptional Case: parameters of faith in the modern world* (London: Darton Longman & Todd, 2002).

President Sarkozy of France has begun speaking about the need for "a positive secularism". He said, on the occasion of Pope Benedict's visit to France, "It would be crazy to deprive ourselves of religion; [it would be] a failing against culture and against thought. For this reason, I am calling for a positive secularity... A positive secularity offers our consciences the possibility to interchange – above and beyond our beliefs and rites – the sense we want to give to our lives." And he concluded, "Positive secularism, open secularism, is an invitation to dialogue, to tolerance and respect."[3]

Many people who claim not to believe in God take a similar view to Nick Clegg, the leader of the Liberal Democrat Party in Britain, who said in an interview shortly after being elected leader, "I'm not some rabid atheist by any stretch of the imagination. If anything, I feel almost inadequate that I don't have faith".[4] Mr Clegg's honesty and humility is a good reminder to believers of all faiths that faith itself is a gift and, for reasons that we can never understand, God doesn't give this gift of explicit faith to everyone. God's redemptive love includes the whole of humanity. God joined the human race and became human in the Incarnation of the Son of God. Those of us who have faith live and work with those who haven't: in the light of our faith we recognise in them the deepest truth of their identity, which is that they share with us the dignity of being sons and daughters of God.

Being "spiritual" versus being "religious"

Today it is widely recognised that being spiritual does not necessarily imply being religious. Indeed, there is a tendency to contrast, rather unfavourably, spirituality with religion. Spirituality is seen as pure and wholesome, liberating and healing, while religion is often seen as ritualistic and formalistic, narrowly moralistic, with an ever-present tendency to being oppressively legalistic. While this may have had, at times, a "grain" of truth, it is a gross caricature

---

3 "Sarkozy: It's crazy to take religion out of society" *Zenit: The world seen from Rome* [Online news agency] (12 Sep 2008) <http://www.zenit.org/article-23608?l=english>, accessed 17 Apr. 2009.

4 Simon Barrow, "Starting afresh", *Third Way*, May 2008, 20.

of religion. It is comparing what is best in spirituality with what is most unhealthy or distorted in the religious practices of some individuals. If we want to compare spirituality with religion we should compare the best in the one with the best in the other.

The contrast between the spiritual and the religious is far too simplistic and naive. Without the revelation that comes to us through our Christian faith, the spiritual dimension is all-too-easily merged with the psychological. And then people begin to believe that there is nothing else there but the psychological. As one writer points out:

> The important thing here is to realize that my depth is deeper than I am. But at the same time I may plunge into myself and never find anything more than myself. The self, in fact, is so deep that it can engulf me without my ever realizing there is something further. It is easy to see why so many mystics lose themselves in themselves and never meet God.[5]

Human reason by itself cannot know the depth of the spiritual or the inner nature of God: only God can reveal God. Human wisdom today seeks to dominate all discussion of our social and family life as well as health care. Secular humanists simply refuse to admit that for centuries, long before Government became involved, the only agencies delivering these services were Church-sponsored bodies. In Britain and Europe the State has been playing catch-up with the Church as far as education, adoption, and the care of sick and elderly people are concerned, and in recent years we have seen a small group of secularists seeking to marginalise the Church and force Catholic agencies to either abandon their Catholic ethos and ethic or abandon their work. But the whole lesson of history teaches us that the society that tries to banish God begins very quickly to banish the human beings that are deemed outsiders or unacceptable. Intolerance of faith leads to denial of humanity. Witness the terrible

---

5   Harvey D. Egan, *Christian Mysticism: the future of a tradition* (New York: Pueblo Publishing Co., 1984), 249.

history of Nazism, Stalinism, Maoism and the many other atheistic and totalitarian regimes of the twentieth century. Speaking to young people in Australia, Pope Benedict said:

> There are many today who claim that God should be left on the sidelines, and that religion and faith, while fine for individuals, should either be excluded from the public forum altogether or included only in the pursuit of limited pragmatic goals. This secularist vision seeks to explain human life and shape society with little or no reference to the Creator. It presents itself as neutral, impartial and inclusive of everyone. But in reality, like every ideology, secularism imposes a world-view. If God is irrelevant to public life, then society will be shaped in a godless image.[6]

A healthy spirituality will always yearn for the truth and seek true answers to life's deepest questions: What is humanity? What is the meaning of human life, of the love and the joy, of the suffering and evil and of death itself that confronts each person in this world? Christians live the answer to these profound questions because Christianity itself is about the meaning of life.

The leitmotif of Christian spirituality is one of amazement at the dignity of human beings. This amazement fills us with joy in the realisation of being the beloved and redeemed sons and daughters of God. And, knowing who we are in the presence of God, we are filled with a living hope in the resurrection of the body and life everlasting. Pope John Paul II said in his first encyclical, "In reality, the name for that deep amazement at man's worth and dignity is the Gospel, that is to say: the Good News. It is also called Christianity. This amazement determines the Church's mission in the world and, perhaps even more so, 'in the modern world'."[7] What a profound

---

6 Pope Benedict XVI, "Welcoming celebration by the young people in Bangaroo", *Travels* [online archive] 17 July 2008, <http://www.vatican.va/holy_father/benedict_xvi/travels/2008/index_australia_en.htm>, accessed 23 Apr. 2009.

7 John Paul II, *Redemptor Hominis* [The Redeemer of Man], 10.

and exciting way of seeing the Gospel. The Gospel is about us, about who we are, and not just about God. With its good news about us, the Gospel is the real source of our joy and happiness in this world. It is a Gospel of joy for the human race.

Our core beliefs: source of our joy

A joyless religion that does not celebrate who the human person is, but focuses narrowly and negatively on what the person must do and how they fail or sin, will quickly become irrelevant for people today. But the Christian faith should never be presented in that way. Consider, for instance, some of the basic beliefs we hold about ourselves. We are:

- created in the image and likeness of God *(Genesis 1:26)*
- fallen but restored *(Genesis 3 and 2 Corinthians 5:17)*
- precious in God's sight *(Isaiah 43:4)*
- little less than a god and crowned with glory and beauty *(Psalm 8:5)*
- reborn of water and the Holy Spirit *(John 3:6)*
- God's temple *(1 Corinthians 3:16)*
- temple of the Holy Spirit *(1 Corinthians 6:19)*
- the body of Christ *(1 Corinthians 12:27)*.

Truly, as Pope John Paul said, the Gospel is the "amazement at human dignity". This amazement is the source of joy in life, joy in being human, joy in being oneself. St Paul lists joy as the second fruit of the Holy Spirit. Joy flowing from love is the characteristic mark of the Christian. We tell the whole world about this joy at Mass when we describe our condition as "waiting in joyful hope for the coming of our Saviour, Jesus Christ". Commenting on the words the angel spoke to Mary, Pope Benedict pointed out that "the first word of the New Testament is an invitation to joy".[8] Mary acted

---

8   Pope Benedict XVI, "Pastoral visit to the Roman Parish of Santa Maria Consolatrice" in *Homilies* [online archive] 18 Dec. 2005, <http://www.vatican.va/holy_father/benedict_xvi/homilies/index_en.htm>, accessed 20 Apr. 2009.

on that invitation. She told us in her magnificent song, "My soul glorifies the Lord and my spirit rejoices in God my Saviour" (Luke 1:46-47). As disciples of Christ we are called to share in Christ's own joy. Jesus said, "I have told you this so that my own joy may be in you and your joy may be complete" (John 15:11).

The amazement at human dignity, at what God has done in us, fills the heart with joy, a joy that the troubles of this world cannot destroy. As I write these words my sister Celia is terminally ill with brain cancer and may die at any moment. I have been celebrating Mass in her house, with her family, and she has been participating with great faith and fervour. We are all choked up with sadness and the tears can flow at any moment. But beneath all the sadness and grief there is stillness, a faith-inspired assurance that, far from ending, her beautiful life is coming to its ultimate fulfilment in God. Even in her state of total weakness and exhaustion her gentleness and graciousness shine through. Her constant word is "thank you". Our grief and sadness at her approaching departure from us in this life is made bearable by the deep joy in knowing that her life is not "being cut short" but being fulfilled. St Paul said, "Do not grieve... like those who have no hope" (1 Thessalonians 4:13). We are grieving in hope, the sure hope of the resurrection. That is the ultimate ground for joy, a joy that even death cannot take away. Joy, as St Augustine said, flows from truth: "That is the authentic happy life, to set one's joy on you, grounded in you and caused by you... The happy life is joy based on the truth. This is joy grounded in you, O God, who are the truth".[9]

Joy needs truth for its sure foundation. As Augustine said so succinctly in his beautiful Latin phrase, *gaudium de veritate,* it is "joy from the truth". Without truth the human mind lives in darkness and confusion and is ultimately filled with fear and anxiety. Without truth the human mind tries to find meaning in transient things, in distractions, or escapism, or some other form of denial of reality. Our Christian faith gives us the truth that is

---

9   St Augustine, *Confessions*, 10, 23.

the sure foundation of our hope and joy. Our faith in the Gospel of Christ fills us with "amazement at human dignity".

In his very fine study of the writings of Pope Benedict, Mgr Joseph Murphy has shown that joy is the recurring theme in all Cardinal Ratzinger's voluminous writings both before and after he was elected pope. The Christian life is a vocation to joy, true joy in God. In our world so lacking in joy, Pope Benedict is convinced that the reawakening of joy in God, joy in God's revelation and in friendship with God is an urgent task for the Church in our century. Joseph Murphy himself writes, "Joy, like love, is at the heart of what it means to be Christian, and it testifies to the conviction that human life has an ultimate meaning revealed to us by God and guaranteed by his unfailing love. The Christian message, the Gospel or 'glad tidings', reveals the path to the lasting joy that satisfies the deepest needs of the human heart."[10] The angels proclaimed this joy to the shepherds at the birth of Christ, "I bring you news of great joy, a joy to be shared by all the people" (Luke 2:10).

Knowing the truth about ourselves, the truth that Jesus alone can reveal to us, enables us gratefully to accept ourselves from the creative love of God the Father; it makes it possible for us to put our trust in Jesus Christ, his only Son; it also gives us the capacity to welcome the gift of the Holy Spirit. Our faith opens the door of joy and peace for us. But we must enter through that door and not just sit down outside. Our acceptance of ourselves and others must be active and effective.

In this new edition of *Hallowed Be Thy Name* we will explore some of the profound truths we believe about ourselves. I will seek to share with you the joy with which our faith fills us as we begin to live by God's word to us about ourselves. That is the true source of our spirituality, a spirituality based on the truth of God's word to us. It is that word, the Gospel of Christ, which fills us with joy in the Spirit.

---

10 Msgr Joseph Murphy, *Christ, Our Joy: The theological vision of Pope Benedict XVI* (San Francisco: Ignatius Press, 2008), 3.

My sincere thanks to Redemptorist Publications for publishing this new edition. Thanks to my confrère Fr Tom MacCarte who read the manuscript and spotted lots of misprints. My special thanks to the men and women who have shared their own spiritual experience and spiritual journey with us in these pages. Their stories enrich and inspire our own faith. I am most grateful to them. My last word of thanks goes to the members of my community here at St Mary's. Their friendship and support has made it possible for me to find the time to write this book.

Fr Jim McManus C.Ss.R.
St Mary's
Kinnoull
Perth PH2 7BP

1

Hallowed Be Thy Name

The first big word I ever had to get my tongue around was the word "hallowed". I was blessed to be born into a Catholic home where the family rosary was a nightly prayer. We all joined in, all twelve of us, from the youngest to the oldest. I would be saying my decade and shouting out: "Our Father, who art in heaven, hallowed be thy name." I never asked myself, of course, what this word "hallowed" meant. I had learned the prayer by heart and for years I never thought about the meaning of the words. In fact, throughout my whole life as a priest I don't remember anyone ever asking the meaning of the word.

I learned at an early age that God's name is holy and that we should never take his name in vain. The second commandment, which every child learned at school, states: "You shall not take the name of the Lord your God in vain." Observing this commandment was a serious duty. God's name is a holy name. We must always use it with reverence. Sadly in many "Catholic cultures" there is a habit of using the holy name as an expression of frustration, or fear, or determination. In fact, the most common sin I learned to confess as a boy was "taking the Lord's name in vain". Examples of this sin would be saying "by God I will" or "by Christ I will". Indeed, Catholics have an amazing fluency in introducing the holy name of God or Jesus into quite unholy situations. It is not uncommon to hear Catholics use "Jesus Christ" not as a term of reverence but as an expletive.

We are not concerned here, however, with the abuse of the holy name; we are concerned with "hallowing" God's name. When we pray "hallowed be thy name" what exactly are we talking about? Are we asking that we ourselves will always refrain from taking God's name in vain by avoiding any colloquial abuse of the holy name? Are we asking that we hallow God's name by refraining from any behavioural abuse, living in a way that is contrary to God's holiness? Are we asking that God himself hallow his name by coming to save us from our sins?

Since God is all holy and his name is holy how could we "hallow" his name? The more we think about this the more clearly we will see that we cannot. Although we can abuse his name, we ourselves cannot make it holy. God alone can make his own name holy. Gerard Lohfink's comments were a great enlightenment to me. He asks:

> What is really meant by the prayer, now so strange to us, that God sanctify his name? Once again the answer is given in the Old Testament, in Ezekiel 36. There it is said that the name of God has been desecrated by the dispersal of Israel among the nations. As a result of this, all the nations say: "So this is the people of God! This Yahweh must be a miserable God, if he is unable to preserve his own people from the loss of their land" (cf. Ezekiel 36:20). In this situation God speaks through Ezekiel: He says, "But I have been concerned about my holy name, which the House of Israel has profaned among the nations where they have gone. And so, say to the House of Israel, 'The Lord Yahweh says this: I am not doing this for your sake, House of Israel, but for the sake of my holy

name, which you have profaned among the nations where you have gone. I mean to display the holiness of my great name, which has been profaned among the nations, which you have profaned among them. And the nations will learn that I am Yahweh – it is the Lord Yahweh who speaks – when I display my holiness for your sake before their eyes. Then I am going to take you from among the nations and gather you together from all the foreign countries, and bring you home to your own land'" (Ezekiel 36:23-25). The text clearly shows that *God himself* will sanctify his name.[1]

God's name will be "hallowed" or "sanctified" when he saves and delivers his people from their exile and dispersal among the nations of the world. He will bring them "home to their own land". He will restore them, not just to the land of the promise, but he will fulfil in them the promise that he made to their ancestors: he will be their God and they will be his people. His promise (in Ezekiel 36:24-29) is packed full of action verbs and bodily images:

- I am going to take you… and gather you together
- I shall pour clean water over you
- I shall cleanse you
- I shall give you a new heart
- and put a new spirit in you
- I shall remove the heart of stone… and give you a heart of flesh
- I shall put my spirit in you
- you shall be my people and I will be your God.

Each one of those great promises contains in itself the whole work of our salvation. When we say "hallowed be thy name" we are saying, "Pour clean water over us, give us a new heart, put your spirit in us". It is clearly God himself who hallows God's name.

---

1 Gerhard Lohfink, *Jesus and Community: the social dimension of Christian faith,* trans. John P. Galvin (London: SPCK, 1985), 15.

Notice the physical and bodily dimension of God's work of hallowing. The Bible never "spiritualises" God's work. The clean water is poured over our bodies and we are cleansed. To understand what God is doing we have to have a great appreciation of our bodies. It is in and through our bodies that God sanctifies us. It is from within our bodies that the "heart of stone" is removed and replaced with a "heart of flesh". This great promise anticipates St Paul's yearning "for the redemption of the body" (Romans 8:23). Christian faith is not a belief in the "immortality of the soul" but in the "redemption of the body", indeed in the "resurrection of the body".

The "redemption of our bodies" begins in this world as God "hallows his name" in our whole human reality of body and soul: in our senses and emotions; in our intellect and will; in our sensuality and our spirituality. The Word of God, as St John tells us, "became flesh" and in that wonderful mystery of God's love "all flesh" was hallowed and redeemed. As we contemplate the Son of God becoming a human being like us, being conceived in his mother's womb and being born with our flesh and blood, there can be no doubt about God's love for what is human. God has become human. St Athanasius, commenting on the implications of the incarnation for our own bodies, wrote in the fourth century:

> The human body has been greatly enhanced through fellowship and union of the Word with it. From being mortal, it has become immortal; though physical, it has become spiritual; though made of earth, it has passed through the gates of heaven.[2]

St Athanasius' high esteem of the human body was inspired by his faith in the incarnation of the Son. He eschewed the dualistic attitudes, so prevalent in his time, which divided the human being into body and soul, seeing all dignity in the soul while devaluing the body. That dualistic separation of body and soul has plagued

---

2 Office of Readings, 1st January.

Christianity throughout the centuries and can still be active in the way people see their bodies. Pope Benedict XVI referred to this negativity towards the body in his first encyclical *God Is Love*. He wrote:

> Nowadays, Christianity of the past is often criticised as having been opposed to the body; and it is quite true that tendencies of this sort have always existed. Yet the contemporary way of exalting the body is deceptive. *Eros,* reduced to pure sex, has become a commodity.[3]

The true beauty and dignity of the human body are often lost sight of in a base urge for pleasure and entertainment. The very fallacious dictum, "It is only my body and I can do what I like with or to my body" is often used to justify all kinds of abuses of the body. People adopt an attitude towards their body which they would not adopt towards their person. Nobody would say, "It is only my person". They would rightly demand respect for their person at all times. But you cannot separate your body from yourself. Indeed, in his wonderful teaching on the theology of the body, to which we will be constantly referring, John Paul II said:

> What is at issue is not only the body (understood as an organism in the "somatic" sense) but also *man who expresses himself by means of that body,* and in this sense, I would say, "is" that body. And he concludes, "The body is permeated above all (if one may express it this way) by the whole reality of the person and its dignity."[4]

God hallows his name by doing a great work in us, by making us holy. It is your whole being, your body-person, that God makes holy. As St Paul said:

---

3 Pope Benedict XVI, *Deus Caritas Est* [God is Love], 5.

4 Pope John Paul II, *Man and Woman: He Created Them: A Theology of the Body* (Boston, MA: Pauline Books and Media, 2006), 55:2&4.

> Your body, you know, is the temple of the Holy Spirit, who is in you since you received him from God. You are not your own property; you have been bought and paid for. That is why you should use your body for the glory of God (1 Corinthians 6:19).

This was how the early Church understood this prayer. The great African father of the Church, Tertullian, writing in the third century said:

> When we say "hallowed by thy name", we ask that it should be hallowed in us, who are in him; but also in others whom God's grace still awaits, that we may obey the precept that obliges us to pray for everyone, even our enemies. That is why we do not say expressly hallowed be thy name "in us", for we ask that it be so in all men.[5]

When we pray "hallowed by thy name" we are saying "save thy people, Lord". "Hallowed be thy name" sums up everything that Jesus wants the Father to do in us. Jesus wants the Father to save us, to sanctify us, to protect us from all evil. When you are worried about your family, or your loved ones, you couldn't say a better prayer than "hallowed be thy name". It contains every good thing that you could possibly wish for them. This is a simple way to pray about any problem: you think of the problem, you offer the problem to God and you say "Father, hallowed be thy name". St Alphonsus Liguori, a great doctor of prayer, encouraged people to share with God all their thoughts of fear or of sadness in an intimate and personal way. Then leave all with God. We don't have to tell God what to do about the problem. In asking God to hallow his name we are asking him to save, sanctify, protect and deliver. Pope John Paul writes: "To save means to embrace and lift up with redemptive love, with love that is always greater than any sin."[6] When we pray

---

5   *Catechism of the Catholic Church*, 2814.

6   Pope John Paul II, *Crossing the Threshold of Hope* (London: Jonathan Cape, 1994), 58.

"hallowed be thy name" over our problems we are asking God to embrace and lift us up in his redemptive love.

Our prayer to God, "hallowed be thy name", is the very source of our spiritual life because if God doesn't hallow his name in us we will have no life. Jane, a former course participant, and not her real name, gave her testimony about how she experienced God hallowing his name in her own life. Jane had had a relationship with a married man which had left her pregnant. Three months into the pregnancy Jane had an abortion, and had been running away from the emotional and psychological effects of this ever since. On arriving at the renewal centre, Jane was encouraged gently to face her story. She says:

> I know it meant I had to unload a huge story, a story too big for me, a story wrapped in fear and guilt and somehow sealed with silence. I had a long healing journey to make. I was struggling with God's interest in an unlovable creature like me, but I experienced a very gentle hand of God at work despite the fact that I had divorced God for another relationship which did not work. Very gradually, I learned to accept God's love and forgiveness and to forgive myself. Eventually, I was able to accept the suggestion of naming the child during the celebration of the Eucharist. This was a very special celebration for me, a time when I experienced the powerful presence of a healing and forgiving God. In his peaceful presence I named and received baby Pat. Words alone cannot convey to you the peace and freedom I experienced at that wonderful moment. I spent the night praising God with the words: "Let all that is within me cry worthy." This, for me, was to complete the healing because, in all of it, I would have felt unworthy of what the good Lord was doing for me.

In writing her powerful testimony Jane has become an evangelist. She brings good news, Gospel, from God. Jane has shared with us, with deep faith and utter simplicity, her transforming experience of God. She discovered in her own personal life that it is God himself who hallows his own name and that God displays the holiness of his great name through what he does in us: "I shall pour clean water over you and you will be cleansed... I shall remove the heart of stone from your bodies and give you a heart of flesh... I shall put my spirit in you." Jane's story is so reminiscent of Jesus' own parable of the prodigal son, the son who returned to his father hoping to be accepted as "one of your hired servants". Then he was overwhelmed by the love and acceptance of the father. Jane had a night of prayer and praise with her God. In her pain and isolation Jane had many fears and doubts. In the loving embrace of the Father all doubts vanished. She personally experienced the truth of the words which Pope John Paul addressed to women who have had an abortion:

> The Church is aware of the many factors which may have influenced your decision, and she does not doubt that in many cases it was a painful and even shattering decision. The wound in your heart may not yet have healed. Certainly what happened was and remains terribly wrong. But do not give in to discouragement and do not lose hope. Try to understand what happened and face it honestly. If you have not already done so, give yourself over with humility and trust to repentance. The Father of mercies is ready to give you his forgiveness and his peace in the sacrament of reconciliation. You will come to understand that nothing is definitively lost and you will also be able to ask forgiveness from your child, who is now living in the Lord.[7]

In Jane's case God's name was hallowed when she accepted "forgiveness from her child" and gratefully received baby Pat as her son. Only in the embrace of the Father's love and the forgiveness of the child will the wound in the heart of the mother be healed.

---

7   Pope John Paul II, *Evangelium Vitae* [The Gospel of Life], 99.

In accepting baby Pat, Jane knew the forgiveness of her child. She had returned and she knew she was totally accepted. That divine acceptance empowered her to accept herself as the mother of baby Pat. Romano Guardini wrote:

> The act of self-acceptance is the root of all things. I must agree to be the person who I am. Agree to have the qualifications which I have. Agree to live within the limitations set for me… The clarity and the courageousness of this acceptance is the foundation of all existence.[8]

Jane agreed to be the person she was, agreed to be mother of the unborn baby. She realised that she had been trying to build her life on the foundation of a twofold denial: the denial of her motherhood and the denial of the personhood of the unborn baby. Such denial may induce a temporary amnesia but it can never bring peace. The reality of her pregnancy meant that she had become a mother and she had conceived a child. Acceptance, not denial is the only true "foundation of all existence". As she accepted her motherhood and named her baby, Jane came into great peace of soul.

The great lie and crippling distortion of our times is that parents can abort a child and live as if nothing has happened. Deep down the expectant mother realises that something dreadful has happened. But women like Jane, who had the great misfortune of conceiving a child in an adulterous relationship, discover, once they turn to God, mercy, compassion and a complete renewal of their lives. Jane had never lost what Pope John Paul beautifully called "the inheritance of the heart". We have been made in God's own image and it was God who gave us life. God has called us and destined us to live in union and communion with him for ever. That is our rich inheritance from God our Father. The inheritance of his own image in our hearts and lives. It is this inheritance, which enables us to respond to the promptings of the Holy Spirit, as Jane did, no matter how far we may have wandered away from God's ways.

---

8 Cited in Leanne Payne, *Restoring the Christian Soul through Healing Prayer* (Eastbourne: Kingsway, 1992), 31.

That was the reality of grace that Jane experienced as God "hallowed his name" in her. As she opened her life to God's word of mercy and forgiveness, the inheritance of her heart, which had been smothered and buried under her sinful failures and self-hatred, became activated and she blossomed again as a beautiful daughter of God. Her spirituality once again became vibrant. But notice, her spirituality was based on the truth of God's love and acceptance, on the truth that she is a beloved and forgiven child of God, and not on some make-believe that nothing bad had happened at all and that she would just get on with her life.

God sent different people to minister to Jane on her journey back to self-acceptance and forgiveness. Each of them prepared her for the liberating moment in the Eucharist when she named and accepted her baby and received God's great forgiveness. The celebration of the Eucharist in thanksgiving for the child, and the committal of the child into the loving hands of God heal the trauma of the abortion. Women who have had abortions will find the peace which Jane found when they build the rest of their lives on the foundation of acceptance: acceptance of the reality of motherhood, acceptance of the human reality of the baby who is now with God and acceptance of the loving forgiveness of God when they turn to him with a contrite heart. They will know, too, in Pope John Paul's words, "the forgiveness of your child, who is now living in the Lord".

Jane had that profound experience of discovering her great dignity as a daughter of God and the mother of her child. She experienced salvation. She experienced the fruit of her prayer "hallowed be thy name". God's name was hallowed in Jane, not by anything she did, but by what he did.

At the close of this chapter I suggest taking a little time to pray over the text of Ezekiel 36 on the new heart. As you prayerfully read this promise, note the following: God's name is hallowed not by what we do, but by what God does. God's name is hallowed when we receive the "new heart". God's name is made holy when we allow God to "pour clean water" over us and cleanse us from all defilement. God's name is hallowed as we gratefully receive "the inheritance of our hearts" and begin to live more consciously.

Personal spiritual exercise

Let us begin by centring ourselves: getting ready for the work of discovering ourselves and our spiritual natures more profoundly:

- Choose a time when you have ten minutes or so to spare. Find a quiet place, somewhere as free of interruptions and disruptions as possible. Sit in a comfortable chair, with your spine upright, your two feet firmly on the floor, your arms relaxed by your side. Close your eyes.
- Feel the tension in your feet and ankles. Let that tension go: let your muscles relax, and feel the tension flow out from your feet and ankles to the earth. Now focus on your legs and do the same thing: feel the tension in the muscles, and let it go: relax and let the tension flow out through your legs to the earth. Now the same thing with your hips, and then your spine, your chest, your arms and hands, your neck. Feel the tension around your jaw, your eyes: let it go, relax, let it flow away through your body and into the earth.
- Notice your breathing. Don't try to change it. Just listen to the rhythms of your body as you relax.
- Notice the sounds that come from outside, and from inside the room. And now go back to paying attention to your breathing.
- Sit quietly like this for a while. What is passing through your mind? Maybe there is nothing there

except stillness. Maybe you have a new sense of the presence of God with you? Or maybe you have some thought or image, or some feeling or emotion. Notice what it is and accept it.

- Now say to God, "Hallowed be thy name", and be still.
- Bring your thoughts back to your breathing and relax.
- And then gradually return to the world.

This technique for deep relaxation may be familiar to you. It is a practice common to many religions, and many non-religious approaches to spiritual questions. It should leave you very calm, and very aware of yourself at many different levels: body, mind, spirit. This is an excellent place from which to start our work of exploring Christian spirituality – from the stillness of your heart to the stillness of the heart of God. It is also one of the oldest forms of prayer: the oldest form of Christian prayer which we call "centring" prayer. At the end of each chapter I will invite you to enter into this practice.

2

Living by the Word of God

In her long night of prayer, as she praised God with "all that is within", Jane found that she experienced a profound healing. She also discovered the truth that "humans do not live on bread alone but on every word that comes from the mouth of God" (Matthew 4:4). The gift of the new heart, which we seek as we pray "hallowed be thy name", enables us to hear the word of God, to accept it and begin to live by it.

Each of us has had the experience of living by a word. Sometimes, of course, we have never reflected on this experience. Recall, for instance, an occasion when you were feeling in great form: everything was going well, you had no worries, the family were well and you had good friends. Then, out of the blue, a person whom you considered a good friend said something, or did something, nasty to you. What happened? You probably spent the rest of the day thinking about it, worrying about it, getting mad about it. Your whole mood changed. From feeling elated you began to feel deflated. That is the power of the human word. It can build up or it can pull down; it can elate or deflate; it can encourage or discourage. I like to use the image of "landing rights". When that awful war was waged against Iraq, the British and American governments needed "landing rights" before they could land their warplanes in other countries in order to refuel. They even needed rights to fly over other countries, to enter their airspace, in order to attack Iraq. We tend to give "landing rights" to our hearts to whoever wants to speak a nasty word to us. We allow the nasty word to fly from a person's mouth, land on our hearts and disturb our inner peace. Why should we do such a silly thing? Our motto should be, "no landing rights to our hearts for the nasty and the negative."

Our protection against the destructive, sinful human word is the creative, liberating word of God. We must consciously choose that protection. For instance, God says, "You are precious in my sight" (Isaiah 43:4) but an inner voice may say, "You are useless". Which voice do you believe? If we wish, we can ignore God's word and live simply by the negative human word.

In this chapter we want to consider some of the implications of living by God's word. But first of all, we have to consider what is involved in living by the word.

Formation of self-image

Our self-image is formed by a word: the most profound influence the word exercises in our life. None of us is born with a self-image. When a baby is born it has no awareness of being separate from its mother. It gradually becomes aware of its separate identity. The identity which the baby begins to form is at the mercy of the word spoken to it: beautiful or ugly, welcome or unwelcome, a joy or a nuisance.

As the words of love or rejection, of affirmation or repudiation enter into the child's consciousness, its self-image begins to be formed. The child will grow up as a confident, assured young person, capable of trusting and reaching out in love to others, or as an insecure, self-centred person, incapable of reaching out in real love. Parents are becoming more and more aware of the need to speak lovingly and positively to their children.

In this chapter, however, we are not concerned with the words which parents and family speak to young children. We are concerned with the words which we as adults speak to ourselves. We are concerned with our self-talk that we engage in all day long. What are we saying to ourselves about ourselves? Are we proclaiming God's liberating word of love and acceptance or are we speaking our own sinful word of condemnation and rejection?

Our true identity

Our real identity is not revealed by finding out who we are in our own sinful eyes, or the eyes of others, but in coming to understand who we are in God's loving and forgiving eyes.

Notice the double revelation that Christ gives us. He simultaneously reveals to us that God is our loving Father and that we are God's beloved sons and daughters. Christ alone can fully reveal us to ourselves. He alone can reveal the mystery of our deepest identity as God's beloved children. This revelation is the source of our spirituality. When we live by this revelation we are living our deepest identity, living the mystery of our true selves. And, as Anselm Gruen wrote, our true self is a very deep mystery:

> My true self is a mystery because it is God expressing himself in a unique way. It is the original image that God shaped of me. It is the unique word of God that is intended, longs, and strives to become flesh in me. My self is the word that is intended to come into the world through me and in me, and to be born as my true self. My spiritual self is this unique and inimitable word of God that longs and throbs in its longing to be made visible and audible in me alone.[1]

Christian spirituality, if it is to remain healthy, must be constantly renewed and re-grounded in this mystery of who we are as God's children. We read in chapter one about Jane, and how she struggled

---

1 Anselm Gruen, *The Spirit of Self-esteem*, trans. John Cumming (Tunbridge Wells: Burns & Oates, 2000), 26.

to make this discovery. Because she was acutely aware of her adulterous relationship and the abortion, Jane condemned herself, hated herself and even contemplated destroying herself. Jane had to learn that the right response to sinful weakness is not self-hatred but repentance, not self-condemnation but the entrustment of self to the mercy and compassion of God. How sad it is that when a person sins grievously the biggest temptation is to reject and condemn self and maybe, like Jane, to spend years doing that. God is saying the very opposite: "Come now, let us talk this over, says the Lord. Though your sins are like scarlet, they shall be as white as snow; though they are red as crimson, they shall be like wool" (Isaiah 1:18).

Until Jane opened her heart in total confidence to God her self-image was being formed by the destructive word of shame and guilt, and not by the creative word of God. She used the colourful phrase "I had locked myself up in fear, shame and guilt" to describe that inner house in which she dwelt. Her phrase for her captivity evokes Jesus' image for true freedom: "If you make my word your home you will indeed be my disciples, you will learn the truth and the truth will make you free" (John 8:31-32).

As her merciful Father completed her liberation from her prison of hate and despair during the Mass she found her true home in God's word. She spent the whole night before God praying, "let all that is within me cry worthy". And she recognised the providential significance of this. She wrote, "This, for me, was to complete the healing, because in all of it, I would have felt unworthy of what the good Lord was doing in me."

Jane had lived so long in that prison of the destructive word, condemning herself even though she was sorry for her sins, that she found it difficult to believe that God could love or esteem her. She needed the whole night in prayer to enter into true freedom. In the Mass, that afternoon, we gave a lot of time to the prayer "We thank you for counting us worthy to stand in your presence and serve you." It is God alone who declares us worthy. Jane filled the whole night with that prayer. Jane discovered the truth about God, revealed in the prophet Isaiah:

> Let them return to the Lord, that he may have mercy on
>   them,
> and to our God, for he will abundantly pardon.
> For my thoughts are not your thoughts,
> nor are my ways your ways, says the Lord.
> For as the heavens are higher than the earth,
> so are my ways higher than your ways
> and my thoughts than your thoughts (55:7-9).

The image of two houses

In the Bible we have two striking yet different images of "houses" in which we can make our home. Jesus invites us to make our home in his word: "If you continue in my word, you are truly my disciples" (John 8:31). In the psalms we are warned about the destructive word: "You love all words that devour, O deceitful tongue" (Psalm 52:4).

If our self-image is formed in the house of the destructive word we will have a very poor self-image. We will have a low self-esteem and a low esteem of everyone else as well. If we discover that we have taken up residence in the house of the destructive word, if we find that we are negative about ourselves and others, then it is most urgent that we vacate that house immediately. We must do a moonlight flit, abandon the house of the destructive word and make our home in God's word. That escape from the house of the destructive word is a good image of inner healing.

Inner healing is the experience of the healing love of God in which the person realises that self is loveable (healing of the self-image) or that self can love and forgive others (healing of relationships) or that self can gratefully integrate some painful past event into the present (healing of memories). Each of these healings comes through faithfully living by the word of God. We will consider each type of healing in turn.

Healing of self-image

All healing comes through the word of God. As we live by the word that God speaks for our healing, we escape the prison of the destructive word. When God made us he modelled us on himself – his own image and likeness. You may have been enchanted by beautiful scenery, enthralled by wonderful sunsets, inspired by great works of art, but nothing in all creation, no matter how beautiful, is more like God than yourself. As scripture says, "We are God's work of art, created in Christ Jesus, to live the good life as he intended us to live it from the beginning" (Ephesians 2:10). We are God's work of art and not trash or rubbish as our sins would have us believe. And, even at our most sinful, we remain God's work of art. What a healing revelation!

God not only tells us that he created us in his own image and likeness; he tells us how he feels about us. He says, "You are precious in my sight and I love you and give you honour. Do not be afraid I have redeemed you" (Isaiah 43:1. 4). How do you feel in the presence of someone who keeps telling you that you are precious in his or her sight? God keeps telling us, "I have loved you with an everlasting love" (Jeremiah 31:3). God addressed all our emotions. Three hundred and sixty-six times God tells us not to fear, that we will not be put to shame (Psalm 71:1), that he will protect us and deliver us (Psalm 109:21), that we are the apple of his eye (Zechariah 2:8), that he exults with joy over us. As we go through the Bible we find hundreds of Divine protestations of undying love. The one that sums up all the others is surely Christ's own words: "God loved the world so much that he gave up his only Son, so that everyone who believes in him may not be lost but may have eternal life" (John 3:16).

So often there is a massive discrepancy between the word God speaks to us about ourselves and the way we feel about ourselves. God says we are redeemed, we feel we are lost; God says he loves us with an everlasting love, we feel that God has never loved us at all; God says we are precious in his sight, we feel that we are of very little value to him; God says that he will give us a new heart and put a new spirit in us, we feel God can do nothing for us.

The reality of sin

We cannot make sense of our human experience without confronting the reality of sin. Sin exists because of the freedom we enjoy in our relationship with God and one another. We have been created for a life of union with God and we can use our freedom to choose a life apart from God. We choose this separation because we believe an illusion, the illusion that living outside God's law will bring us freedom and happiness. We were created to love and to live in a union of communion with others. But love, which is a free gift of self to the beloved, often evades us. Instead of making a sincere gift of self to the other we so often engage in self-seeking, or looking for self-gratification from the other. While love always personalises, sin always objectifies; love is self-giving, sin is self-seeking; love sees the person to whom one wishes to make the gift of self, sin sees in the person an object for its own advantage or gratification.

The experience of sin brings the very opposite of happiness: fear, unhappiness, lack of freedom. Scripture says, "The law of the Lord is perfect, it gives life to the soul" (Psalm 19:7). The illusion of sin says if you want real life ignore the law of the Lord. The discrepancy between what God says to us about ourselves and how we so often feel about ourselves can only be explained by this reality of sin in our lives.

Sin is alienation – alienation from God, neighbour and ourselves. Sin inflicts a wound in the self-image which leads to self-rejection. Conversion of heart brings not only forgiveness of sin but also the healing of the wound of sin.

We confess our sins and we recognise that there can be no human happiness or fulfilment outside the law of God. The decision to live by every word that comes from the mouth of God always involves the decision to live by God's life-giving commandments. Agnes Stanford used to say that when we speak of sin as "breaking

God's law" we are not speaking correctly. If a man, she said, steps off the top of a precipice he doesn't break the law of gravity; he just demonstrates it. If we collide with the divine law that collision will not break the law, it will break us. When we sin we offend God. But we also inflict a wound on our innermost being. And for that we need healing. When others sin against us, their cruel words or deeds inflict wounds on us. For those wounds too we need inner healing. Sometimes we might be unconsciously living out of the pain of those wounds.

The following panel helps us to contrast the choice before us each day. We can live by the negative word that comes through the wound of sin or we can live by the creative word that comes from our core beliefs:

Manifestations of the wound of sin	Manifestations of core beliefs
Self-rejection	Image of God (Genesis 1:26)
Self-hatred	Precious in God's sight (Isaiah 43:4)
Fear	I am with you always (Matthew 28:20)
Poor self image	God's work of art (Ephesians 2:10)
Guilt	Your body is the temple of the Holy Spirit (1 Corinthians 6:19)
Shame	You are Christ's body (1 Corinthians 12)

The wound of sin in the self-image leads to self-rejection. The healing of that wound comes through the grace of self-acceptance. Self-acceptance, as Guardini said, is "the foundation of all existence". It is the goal of Christian existence. It is not there by birth, but by our rebirth. As St Peter said, "your new birth was not from any mortal seed but from the everlasting word of the living and eternal God" (1 Peter 1:23). If we wish to form our self-image by the word of God we must begin, like Mary the mother of Jesus, to "ponder God's word" in our hearts.

Our self-image must be formed by the divine words of affirmation and encouragement we have received. The healing of our self-image takes place, and God's name is hallowed, as we confess our sins, ask God's pardon and then humbly begin to make God's word our home and forsake that house of the destructive word.[2]

Healing of relationships

Living by the word of God, by the word of forgiveness, is the only way to experience healing for the inner wounds which are inflicted on us in our ordinary relationships with friends and acquaintances. Our instinct, when hurt, is to get even, to get revenge. St Peter asked Jesus, "Lord, how often must I forgive my brother if he wrongs me? As often as seven times? Jesus answered, not seven times, I tell you, but seventy seven times" (Matthew 18:21). The word of God asks us to offer unconditional forgiveness; the word of our own hurt instinct asks for revenge. It is a choice between the word of God, which is the wisdom of God, or the word of our hurt feelings, which is the wisdom of this world. Jesus asks us to forgive unconditionally because he is the man who, from the cross, could pray "Father forgive them, they do not know what they are doing" (Luke 23:34).

Judged by the wisdom of this world, unconditional forgiveness is folly, but it belongs to the "folly of the cross". It is the crucified Jesus, the God-man who was insulted, betrayed, rejected and finally executed on a cross, who teaches us to forgive unconditionally, who tells us to love our enemies. Christ's teaching on unconditional forgiveness has never been popular. It is only when we firmly believe that the "crucified Christ" is the "power of God and the wisdom of God" that we will be able to proclaim that unconditional forgiveness too is the wisdom of God. Such forgiveness takes its meaning from the cross. We cannot harmonise in our faith an

---

2 For a full discussion of the healing of the self-image and inner healing see my books, *Healing in the Spirit* (Chawton: Redemptorist Publications, 2002) and *The Healing Power of the Sacraments* (2005).

acceptance of the crucified Christ with a rejection of his words "Father forgive". The quality of my faith acceptance of Christ crucified, the wounded, suffering, dying Jesus, is clearly manifested in the quality of the unconditional forgiveness which I offer to a brother or a sister. Through forgiving we truly accept the Christ who was wounded and died for us and we experience the truth proclaimed in scripture: "By his wounds you have been healed." (1 Peter 2:24; see also Isaiah 53:5). Unconditional forgiveness heals the broken heart. C. S. Lewis wrote:

> There is all the difference in the world between forgiving and excusing. Forgiveness says, "Yes, you have done this thing, but I accept your apology, I will never hold it against you and everything between us two will be exactly the same as it was before." But excusing says, "I see that you couldn't help it, or didn't mean it, you weren't really to blame." If one was not really to blame then there is nothing to forgive. In this sense forgiveness and excusing are almost opposite.[3]

When we forgive from our heart we are exercising the mighty power of God's word, living by God's word, and through that word the broken heart is healed. God has put into the human heart the self-healing power of forgiveness. And when we use this power to forgive we experience deep healing in our relationships with others. Common sense tells us that holding grudges or resentments can never be good for us.

In our own time psychologists and medical scientists have begun to discover the healing power of forgiveness. Dr Luskin has worked with people from troubled parts of the world. He has brought groups of Catholic and Protestant women from Belfast to Stanford University to go through his forgiveness programme. They had one thing in common: each of them had lost either a son or a husband through the violence in Northern Ireland. On arrival

---

3   C.S. Lewis, *Fern-Seed and Elephants and Other Essays on Christianity* (London: Fount, 1975), 40.

they had a medical check-up and at the end of the programme they had another medical check-up. This is how he describes the results:

> On the measure of how hurt the Irish women felt by their loss, on a scale of 1 to 10, they began the week with a score near 8.5. Again, this is a simple, standard psychological test where each woman draws a line across a page to represent her current level of pain. When they left at the end of the week, they registered their hurt a bit over 3.5. When the questionnaires were returned at the six-month follow-up, their hurt score still stood below 4.
>
> On a separate measure, that of stress, the women reduced their stress by almost half from the beginning of the training to the follow-up six months later.
>
> These Irish women showed an increase in forgiveness toward the person who had committed the murder, of about 40 percent over the week of the training. This positive result remained constant at the follow-up evaluation. Their depression scores also improved. Given a list of 30 items indicating depression, the women checked an average of 17 at the beginning, an average of 7 at the end of the training, and 10 at the six-month follow-up. The women also showed that by the follow-up assessment they had become significantly more optimistic.[4]

That amazing healing power of forgiveness should not surprise anyone who believes in God's word. God never asks us to do anything that is not for our own good. And the first beneficiary of forgiving is the one who forgives. His or her heart is healed, even if the one they have forgiven wants nothing more to do with them.

In one of her dialogues with God the Father, St Catherine of Sienna asked him what he really thought of the person who forgave a wrong from the heart? God responded: "That person has become

---

4   Dr Fred Luskin, *Forgive for Good* (San Francisco: Harper, 2002), 97.

divine." God's name is truly hallowed in us when we forgive. Unconditional forgiveness is a divine reality. As we enter into this divine reality of unconditional forgiveness we in turn are divinised. When we receive this grace of forgiveness, and when we offer it to the person who has wronged us, we ourselves are "graced" by the divine forgiveness we offer. We become like the Father. That is what Jesus asks when he says "Be compassionate as your heavenly father is compassionate" (Luke 6:36).

We see the power of forgiveness in the life of Nelson Mandela. From the day he was released from prison, the man who was locked up for nearly thirty years as "a violent communist and a dangerous revolutionary" has been preaching the truly revolutionary message of reconciliation, calling on his own people, the oppressed and long-suffering black majority of South Africa, to forgive their white oppressors. Mandela sees clearly that it is not only the oppressed who need liberation; the oppressor is also in need of liberation. Reconciliation is the only road which leads to liberation. In his autobiography he tells us how he fought the spiritual battle to survive as a freedom fighter in prison:

> Prison is designed to break one's spirit and destroy one's resolve. To do this the authorities attempt to exploit every weakness, demolish every initiative, negate all sign of individuality – all with the idea of stamping out that spark that makes each of us human and each of us who we are.[5]

That spark which makes us human is the image of God within us. Mandela understood clearly that if the prison authorities could make him hate they would have broken his spirit. He was a prisoner for justice not for revenge. He tells us about his experience when he stood as a prisoner in the court room where he had, as a lawyer, defended many people:

---

5   Nelson Mandela, *Long Walk to Freedom* (London: Abacus, 1995), 376.

During the proceedings, the magistrate was diffident and uneasy, and would not look at me directly. The other attorneys also seemed embarrassed, and at that moment I had something of a revelation. These men were not only uncomfortable because I was a colleague brought low, but because I was an ordinary man being punished for his beliefs. In a way I had never quite comprehended before, I realised the role I could play in court and the possibilities before me as a defendant. I was a symbol of justice in the court of the oppressor, the representative of the great ideals of freedom, fairness and democracy in a society that dishonoured those virtues. I realised then and there that I could carry on the fight even within the fortress of the enemy.[6]

By keeping his spirit free from bitterness and unforgiveness Mandela did that. For nearly thirty years from prison he inspired the struggle for freedom and justice in South Africa. He remained a free man in prison – free from hatred, from bitterness, from the desire for revenge. This prepared him to become the first president of all South Africans and a great world statesman.[7]

Healing of memories

Sad memories from the past, hidden resentments, even bitterness can be the source of great pain and discouragement. How do we live according to the word of God with regard to the past? How do we relate to our past? The word which God gives us is clear and simple: "Bless the Lord, my soul, bless his holy name, all that is within me! Bless the Lord, my soul, and never forget all his blessings" (Psalm 103:1-2). The word of God invites us to bless God not just with our minds, not just with our hearts or spirits, but with "all that is within". What is within you? Everything that has ever happened to you in your whole life is within you, stored in your memory. The human

---

6 Mandela, *Long Walk to Freedom*, 376.

7 For a detailed analysis of the healing power of forgiveness see my book co-authored with Dr Stephanie Thornton, *Finding Forgiveness: Personal and Spiritual Perspectives* (Chawton: Redemptorist Publications, 2006).

memory is like a computer and every single thing that happens in life is fed into that computer. Most of the events are registered in the subconscious; but every single event is registered. The question is: what are all those tens of thousands of human experiences doing in your life? Each of us can say, "I know that I am the person I am today because of the things which I have lived through". For myself I can say, I am the person I am today because of my parents, my early years in my family, as I grew up; my primary and secondary education; my formation as a priest and a Redemptorist; the forty-five years I have spent in priestly ministry. Those were the major formative influences in my life. There were also deforming influences: my own sinfulness; the discouragement which I experienced from time to time; my failure, at times, to pursue my own on-going formation; the hurts and disappointments and frustrations which are part of life in a fallen world.

With regard to all those experiences, both positive and negative, I have to live according to the word of God. That word directs me to bless God with, in and through all those experiences. It is easy to bless God for the good experiences. But before I can bless God for the bad experiences I need healing. Specifically, I need the healing of memories.

If I find that I am filled with resentment or bitterness as I recall those events I know I am imprisoned in the house of the destructive word. But I don't have to remain locked up there for the rest of my life. Remember Jane and how she experienced total liberation from that destructive word. Remember how she spent that whole night saying, "all that is within me cry worthy". As you begin to live that word and bless God for every single experience of your past life you will experience deep inner healing in your memory. God heals the pain in the memory, not by enabling us to forget, but by enabling us to remember in a new way. As we thank God for all that is within us, for everything that has ever happened in our whole life, the memory becomes grateful. And as we live this gratitude our whole relationship with the past is healed and transformed. Brother Pius, a member of my community, died a few years ago. The day before he died he wrote a long and beautiful letter to all his friends. And he added this PS: "As I look back I have only gratitude".

Healing and liberation come through living by God's word. If the past within me is not blessing God it will be cursing; it will remain un-integrated into my present existence and will be a source of deep unhappiness. I will have bitter and resentful memories. And there is surely nothing worse than becoming a "bitter person". Sadly that can happen. People who have nourished resentments in their memories throughout life can end their days as bitter, sad and angry people.

God wants us to have grateful memories, eucharistic memories. He does not want us to be burdened with resentful memories. Yet, so many people go through life filled with resentments about the past. The word "resent" comes from the Latin word *resentire* which means "to feel again". When we nourish a resentful memory we "feel again" the hurt from the past. It will remain a wound within until it is healed. Time does not heal inner wounds. The only way to have that wound healed is to live by the word of God and say, "All that is within me bless God's holy name". I know from experience that when people are hurting badly they have to struggle to begin relating to their past life with a blessing rather than a curse. But I also know that no one who begins to bless God for "all that is within" fails to come into gratitude and experience a deep healing of memories.

When Jesus says that we don't live "on bread alone but on every word that comes from the mouth of God" he gives us the secret for living in peace – in peace with ourselves because we can pray, "I thank you for the wonder of my being", in peace with our neighbour because we can "forgive seventy times seven" and at peace with our past life because we can pray, "let all that is within me bless God's holy name". As we live by these life-giving words of God we experience inner healing and we become peaceful people. God's name is hallowed.

Personal spiritual exercise

- Centre yourself, using the techniques we learned in the previous chapter.
- Bring yourself to bodily stillness and calm.
- Now try to place yourself truly in the presence of Jesus who reveals who you truly are as a child of God.
- How does it make you feel to be in God's presence as his beloved son or daughter?
- Allow yourself to experience this feeling as powerfully as you can.
- Now focus again on your breathing.
- And bring yourself gently back to the world.

This technique, too, is a very old Christian form of prayer. With perseverance and patience, practicing this form of prayer can lead you to a profound sense of peace: a feeling that you are loveable, just as you are, however that may be.

3

Getting to Know the Word of God

When the Vatican carried out an extensive study on why Catholics were leaving the Catholic Church to join other denominations in the 1980s, it recommended that special attention be given to the experiential dimension of the faith – discovering Christ personally through prayer and dedication, which was the appeal of the charismatic and "born-again" movements.[1] But the real challenge for the Church in our times is not to get our Sunday congregations singing and worshipping in new and more joyful ways – although that is surely most necessary. Nor is the real challenge to get all the faithful actively involved in building up their Christian communities – although that is also vital. The Church's real challenge is that its individual members get to know Christ personally – the knowledge that St Paul craved when he said: "I believe nothing can happen that will outweigh the supreme advantage of knowing Christ Jesus my Lord" (Philippians 3:8).

This personal knowledge of Christ is a precious gift of God – and its starting point is the word of God. St Jerome said that "ignorance of the scriptures is ignorance of Christ", and it is true that most of us

---

1 *Osservatore Romano*, 19 May 1986 (English Edition).

41

need to overcome our basic ignorance of scripture if we're to attain a new level of personal knowledge of Christ.

In order to speak and reveal himself to us, God speaks in human language. We would not understand any other language. The mystery of God's word spoken through human words is similar to the mystery of God acting through human flesh and blood. When Jesus speaks as a man, God is also speaking. In the same way the word of scripture, which we hear proclaimed in church as the human word of St Paul or the prophet Jeremiah, is also the word of God.

Incarnation and inspiration

We call the mystery of God becoming human the mystery of incarnation. We call the mystery of God speaking to us in human words the mystery of inspiration. But that doesn't mean that God dictated the Bible. When Paul sat down to write a letter to the Church at Corinth, he wasn't acting as God's secretary. Paul said what he himself wanted to say. Indeed, to fully understand any of the Bible we have to understand what the human author was saying, which is why the Catholic Church has always held biblical study in high esteem. The study of the sacred texts of scripture – their language, symbolism and historical and cultural context – is vital if each new generation is to interpret God's word for itself. That doesn't mean that only scholars can read the Bible, but they can help us understand the word of God by interpreting the human word. Pope Benedict XVI put it this way:

> Exegesis, the true reading of the holy scripture, is not only a literary phenomenon, not only reading a text. It is the movement of my existence. It is moving towards the word of God in human words. Only by conforming to the mystery of God, to the Lord who is the word, can we enter within the word, can we truly find the word of God in human words.[2]

---

2 Pope Benedict's address to Synod, 8 October 2008.

In 1967 when I joined the staff in our seminary I was amazed to discover that the man who had taught me scripture as a student – a highly qualified biblical scholar – could not accept everything that the Second Vatican Council said about the word of God. While he believed that scripture was the inspired word of God, he could not accept that there was any real comparison between the sacrament of the Lord's body and the proclamation of the word. The "real presence" of Christ in the word should not, in his view, be compared with the "real presence" of Christ in the sacrament. He found "bible services" poor and unacceptable alternatives to rosary and benediction. Yet the Church's position is very clear: "When the scriptures are read in the Church, God himself speaks to his people, and it is Christ, present in his word, who proclaims his Gospel."[3] The bishops of the Second Vatican Council were well aware that for centuries many Catholics had not had any real devotion to the word of God, which is why they wrote: "it is essential to promote that sweet and living love for sacred scripture".[4]

In my training as a theologian I learned to use the scriptures for apologetic purposes. I could prove Catholic doctrine from the scriptures. In a sense the scriptures were a vast quarry from which we learned to hew "proof texts", or useful texts for preaching. We were trained to prove the Church's teaching on the Mass and the sacraments by referring to specific parts of scripture; we could show how the doctrine of the Holy Trinity is revealed in the scriptures; we could demonstrate how the scriptures show that Christ is the Son of God and founded the Church. But we were not trained to have a "sweet and living love" for the scriptures. We were in great need of a renewal in the word of God. And that renewal is now well under way.

This sweet and living love which so many Catholics now have for the word of God is the great grace of renewal which the Holy Spirit has poured out upon the Church through the Second Vatican

---

3 Introduction to the Roman Missal, 9.

4 Second Vatican Council, *Sacrosanctum Concilium* [Constitution on the Sacred Liturgy], 24.

Council. We find this love for the scriptures especially among those who have been touched by renewal in the Spirit. One old priest testified to this grace when he said that before he became involved in renewal in the Spirit, the scriptures in his office book were like a dead letter. Now, he said, "my office book is like a box of chocolates. I am for ever dipping into it."

A busy missionary sister and self-confessed "workaholic" describes how she came to have a love for the scriptures in 1974, when she was on a retreat on the Spiritual Exercises of St Ignatius:

> During the hours of prayer on the scriptures each day the Lord became very close to me. In an overwhelming way, I became aware of his great love for me and I began to realise what I had been missing in my "busy life" heretofore. I resolved that this would change. That was twenty years ago. By God's grace I have not lost my love for the word of God and my periods of prayer are the most important times of the day.

God wants to give each of us that same love for his holy word. But we must give him time.

Love of scripture in the Church today

In his Encyclical letter *For the New Millennium*, John Paul II wrote of the great progress that has taken place since the Second Vatican Council:

> Individuals and communities make extensive use of the Bible, and among lay people there are many who devote themselves to scripture with the valuable help of theological and biblical studies. But it is above all the work of evangelisation and catechesis which is drawing new life from attentiveness to the word of God. Dear brothers and sisters, this development needs to be consolidated and deepened, also by making sure that every family has a Bible. It is especially necessary that

listening to the word of God should become a life-giving encounter, in the ancient and ever valid tradition of *lectio divina*, which draws from the biblical text the living word which questions, directs and shapes our lives.[5]

In 2008, Pope John Paul's dream inspired the Synod of Bishops to devote a whole month to studying how the Church can become more open and alive to the word of God in its midst. Cardinal Marc Quellet of Quebec City summarised the proposals put forward by the Synod. They raise questions as to how to educate people in a living hearing of the word of God at every cultural level; whether it is necessary to revise the lectionary; helping people understand the intrinsic link between the word and the Eucharist; and how to translate and spread the Bible among the greatest possible number of cultures, in particular among the poor.[6] If these proposals are implemented we will experience a new renewal in the Spirit in the Church comparable to that which followed the Second Vatican Council. We can also anticipate a new flourishing in ecumenical relationships, because despite all the doctrinal issues that divide Christians, the word of God unites us.

Lectio divina

Lectio divina literally means divine or holy reading of the scriptures. Pope Benedict is a great advocate of the practice:

> If it is effectively promoted, this practice will bring to the Church – I am convinced of it – a new spiritual springtime. As a strong point of biblical ministry, *lectio divina* should therefore be increasingly encouraged, also through the use of new methods, carefully thought through and in step with the times.[7]

---

5 Pope John Paul II, *At the Beginning of the New Millennium* (London: Catholic Truth Society, 2001), para. 39.

6 The Word seen from Rome <www.zenit.org>

7 Address to the Congress commemorating the fortieth Anniversary of the promulgation of the Constitution on Divine Revelation by the Second Vatican Council, Castel Gandolfo, 16 September 2005.

It developed within the monasteries, and is still an integral part of the spirituality of monks and nuns in the great contemplative orders. In the Carmelite Constitutions we read:

> *Lectio divina* is an authentic source of Christian spirituality recommended by our Rule. We therefore practice it every day, so that we may develop a deep and genuine love for it, and so that we may grow in the surpassing knowledge of Christ. In this way we shall put into practice the apostle Paul's commandment, which is mentioned in our Rule: "Let the sword of the spirit, the word of God, live abundantly in your mouth and in your hearts; and whatever you must do, do it in the name of the Lord."[8]

In practice it is a simple, prayerful approach to listening to the word of God while reading the human word in which it comes. Take a short passage of scripture, read it slowly, and, if appropriate, out loud. This first reading gives a sense of the passage. Then read the whole passage again – slowly, silently and prayerfully. God is speaking to you and so, as you read, ask God to enlighten your heart and let you hear his voice: "If only you would listen to him today, do not harden your hearts" (Psalm 95:7). We listen, not to analyse, but just to hear. As you get a clearer sense of what the word is saying, you begin to ponder it in your heart, in the way that Our Lady "stored up all these things in her heart" (Luke 2:51). Focus all your attention on the word and allow it to illuminate the situation in which you find yourself. Then turn to God with your whole heart and respond to him in praise and thanksgiving, asking for the help you need at that time. Finally, rest in stillness and contemplation, aware that Christ is with you and has spoken to you in his word. Thomas Keating explains this attention to the word in this way:

> As we repeat the phrase or sentence slowly, over and over, a deeper insight may arise. For example, take the words

---

8 *Carmelite Constitutions*, 82.

of Jesus, "I will not call you servants but friends." All of a sudden, it might dawn on us what it means to be a friend of Christ. Our awareness expands without our having done anything but allow the Spirit to act. It is a heart-to-heart exchange with Christ. We think the text but we do not think about the text. If we are thinking in the sense of reflecting, we are dominating the conversation. That can be done fruitfully some other time. Here it is a question of receiving and resting in Christ's presence as the source of the word or phrase.[9]

Commitment to daily reading

Each day we read the scriptures we are hearing God's voice and getting to know Christ in a new way. And conversely, each day we don't open the scriptures is a day when we haven't met the Lord where he wants to meet us – namely, in his word. In our reading we enter into a conversation with God the Father, and it is the source of all prayer and spiritual life. In the words of the Second Vatican Council: "Such is the force and power of the word of God that it can serve the Church as her support and vigour, and the children of the Church as strength for their faith, food for the soul, and a pure and lasting fount of spiritual life."[10] Just as our physical life will not remain strong and robust without our daily food, so our spiritual life will not become strong without our daily visit to the "pure and lasting fount".

Daily scripture reading demands a definite decision and a strong commitment to be faithful to it. We must have a definite time set aside for daily reading. I may have the good intention, but I have discovered over and again that if the time is not fixed, I don't do it. On the other hand, I know when a time is clearly identified as scripture reading time, I do it and enjoy it.

Those who have followed the twelve-week "Hallowed Be Thy Name" spiritual formation programme testify to the same. Part

---

9 Thomas Keating, "The Classical Monastic Practice of Lectio Divina", Contemplative Outreach website (4 Oct. 2008) <http://www.contemplativeoutreach.org/site/News2?page=NewsArticle&id=5253>.

10 Second Vatican Council, *Dei Verbum* [Constitution on Divine Revelation], 21.

of the daily programme is a fifteen-minute Bible reading, which covers the whole of the New Testament over twelve weeks.

Margaret writes about her experience: "It made me more aware of what Our Father wanted to do in my life; it enabled me to reach out to others with love and compassion; it helped all of us to become more Christlike."

Phyllis Gallacher led a small group on one of the programmes: "I found a great response. It encouraged the reading of scripture and prayer... everyone brought their own personal experience and understanding. As time went on we became more open and able to share more deeply."

You might find that you are so enthusiastic about your daily readings that you are tempted to commit more than fifteen minutes to it. But be wary of setting the bar too high, and making commitments you can only keep for a short time. It is better to read fifteen minutes every day for years, than to read an hour for a matter of weeks before "burning out".

Personal spiritual exercise

- Centre yourself, using the techniques we learned in week one.
- Bring yourself to bodily stillness and calm.
- Ask yourself: Do I really believe what God says to me about myself in the Bible? Am I made in the image of God? Am I precious in God's sight?
- Focus again on your breathing.
- Bring yourself gently back to the world.

4

The Word in Prayer

Prayer is talking to God. Long before we get round to praying God has already spoken to us. Our biggest mistake when we pray is to speak to God about ourselves and our needs while ignoring what he has been saying to us.

The old definition of prayer is still valid: prayer is lifting the mind and heart to God. But not to a silent God. We lift our mind and heart to God because we have heard what he says and we want to respond. The Vatican Council's words can be our starting point: "In the sacred scriptures the Father who is in heaven comes lovingly to meet his children and talks with them"[1]. It is the Father who begins the conversation. Recall how Adam, after he had sinned, wanted to escape from God's presence. He didn't want to engage in a conversation with God. But God came looking for him. He called out in the garden, "Where are you?" (Genesis 3:9). It is as if God is asking: "What's the matter; why don't you want to talk to me?" Adam is holding his breath in fear and God takes the initiative: "Where are you?"

---

1 *Dei Verbum*, 21.

49

All human prayer is really a response to that call of God: "Here I am Lord, you have called me", would be a good way to begin any time of prayer. The Vatican Council says: "We speak to God when we pray; we listen to him when we read the scriptures."[2] A good conversationalist is one who has found the right balance between speaking and listening. After a while it's impossible to listen to an incessant talker. And conversely, the non-participation of the silent party makes it almost impossible to hold a conversation. Good prayer, like good conversation, needs both listening and talking. One woman describes how her life was changed by listening to God:

> Before the scriptures came alive for me I never thought that Jesus accepted me as I am with my faults and failings – wanting in so many ways. I felt I could never repay him for his wonderful goodness and patience with me. I was so fearful. The day we gathered for a Prayer Meeting and prayed in groups for each other, expressing our need for healing, a wonderful peace and joy filled me. When again that evening we prayed in silence during Exposition a great peace descended upon me. I felt a different person and wanted to say with the apostles on the mountain: "Lord, it is good for us to be here."

For years she had struggled with her prayers, but she was not comfortable in the Lord's presence because she felt bad about herself and was preoccupied with her own sinfulness. It made heart-to-heart conversation with the Lord impossible, and her prayer was full of duty and fear, lacking warmth, simplicity and love. In other words, she was trying to pray without listening. God had spoken wonderful words of acceptance and love and she had failed to respond. God her Father had said to her: "Because you are precious in my eyes, because you are honoured and I love you... Do not be afraid, for I am with you" (Isaiah 43:4). He had further revealed to her that: "The Lord is merciful and gracious, slow to anger and

---

2 *Dei Verbum*, 25.

abounding in steadfast love" (Psalm 103:8), but she ignored it and lived in fear of non-acceptance. Jesus had said to her: "As the Father has loved me, so I have loved you" (John 15:9), but she hadn't heard him. And Paul had reassured her with the words: "You are not a slave any more" (Galatians 4:7), but she went to her prayer as a slave, in fear of rejection.

We all make this same mistake. So often we go to prayer full of our own fears and anxieties, without listening, even for a moment, to what God is saying to us. But long before we come to our prayer, or conscious awareness of our relationship with God, he has already spoken to us and told us who we are and how much he loves and treasures us. What we are doing is conforming our thoughts to our own fears, instead of God's word. But if I begin my prayer by thinking that God doesn't have much time for me, or that I am awful in his sight, then I am simply denying his word. I am really calling God a liar.

It's hard to sympathise with someone who's groping in the dark, full of fear, if he has simply refused to switch a light on. But we behave like that when we go to pray without the word of God. As the scripture says: "Your word is a lamp to my feet, a light to my path" (Psalm 119:105). If we embark on prayer on the dark roads of life without this lamp we will become afraid, discouraged, and quickly abandon prayer. Our Lord taught this to St Jerome in a remarkable vision. Jerome had left everything to follow the Lord, and was living as a hermit in a cave in Bethlehem. Our Lord appeared to him and said: "Jerome, why don't you give me everything?" Jerome replied: "But Lord, I have given you everything. I gave up my career in Rome and came to live here as a hermit for your sake." The Lord looked lovingly at Jerome and repeated his question: "Jerome, why don't you give me everything?" In some agitation Jerome began to tell the Lord all he had given him: "I gave up my house for you, my career in Rome, I am fasting until sunset and keeping vigils. What more can I give you?" The Lord thanked him kindly and said: "Jerome, why don't you give me your sins?"

The first thing we have to let go of, when we come into God's presence, is our sins. That is why it is so important, when we begin our prayer, to listen to God's word which always invites us to trust him with our sinfulness. As the scriptures say:

> Since in Jesus, the Son of God, we have the supreme high priest who has gone through to the highest heaven, we must never let go of the faith that we have professed. For it is not as if we had a high priest who was incapable of feeling our weaknesses with us; but we have one who has been tempted in every way that we are, though he is without sin. Let us be confident, then, in approaching the throne of grace, that we shall have mercy from him and find grace when we are in need of help (Hebrews 4:14-16).

When we look into our own hearts and become aware of our own sinfulness we hear the words: "Come now, let us talk this over… Though your sins are like scarlet, they shall be as white as snow; though they are red as crimson, they shall be like wool" (Isaiah 1:18). Without listening to the word of God in prayer we simply focus on what is wrong, or on what we need, or on what we have to do. Without listening to God's word we can begin to pray in a way which denies God's great love and mercy. That kind of prayer fills us with fear and anxiety and robs us of peace and joy in God's presence. It is better to pray in the light of God's word than in the darkness of our own fears.

Praying with the scriptures

There are many ways in which we can pray with the scriptures. I recommend three steps, especially while praying for inner healing: acceptance, acknowledgement and allowance.

Acceptance

When we begin our prayer we listen to what God is saying. As Pope Benedict XVI says: "This is what prayer really is – being in silent inward communion with God".[3] In that silent communion God speaks an everlasting word. To each of us God says: "You are precious in my eyes… you are honoured and I love you (Isaiah 43:4). Our first response to this word is to accept it. Acceptance in this sense is not merely intellectual assent. It is, as Pope Benedict says, "conforming my mind to the word"[4]. God says I am precious in his sight. Now my mind conforms to that; that is the truth about me. Acceptance involves total immersion in the word, the type of immersion Jesus refers to when he says: "If you make my word your home you will indeed be my disciples, you will learn the truth and the truth will make you free" (John 8:31-32). Home is where you know who you are. You are a son or daughter of the house and you are accepted. You can relax. The first step in prayer is not simply to hear God's word, but to enter into it, to dwell in it as you do in your own home.

Then, Jesus says, you will receive a new identity: "you will indeed be my disciples". A disciple is one who listens to the master, learns from the master, and tries to please the master. If the master says: "Your sins are forgiven" (Luke 7:49), the disciple gratefully accepts his word. Pope John Paul II describes what is involved in discipleship: "It involves holding fast to the very person of Jesus, partaking of his life and destiny, sharing in his free and loving obedience to the Father. By responding in faith and following the one who is incarnate wisdom, the disciple of Jesus truly becomes a disciple of God."[5]

By identifying with Christ in this total and personal way we receive our new identity as his disciples. As disciples, dwelling in the word as our home, we learn the truth. Truth is not something we acquire through intellectual prowess – we have to learn it. The first condition for learning is docility, that is a willingness to be taught by the master.

---

3 Pope Benedict XVI, *Jesus of Nazareth* (London: Bloomsbury, 2007), 102.

4 As above, 141.

5 John Paul II, *Veritatis Splendor* [The Splendour of Truth], 19.

The Church of Christ, which Paul called "the pillar and bulwark of truth" (1 Timothy 3:15), faithfully interprets his teaching for us. Dwelling in Christ's word always involves dwelling in the Church. The truth is preserved free from all error in the Church because the Church is the Body of Christ. Some people want Jesus without the Church – to hold on to the person of Jesus without holding on to what the Church teaches – but you cannot have Jesus without the Church he established through Peter: "You are Peter and on this rock I will build my Church" (Matthew 16:18).

You will not become precious to God when you become a better or holier person. You couldn't be more precious to God than you are right now. Your first response must be one of acceptance. Accept that this is the deepest truth about yourself in your relationship with God. At the end of a retreat in a large community of sisters, one participant, a woman in her eighties, got up and asked forgiveness from everyone: "All my life I have been like a cat. Anyone who scratched me was scratched back in return. Now I know the reason: I never knew that I was precious in God's sight." That truth set her free to relax in the presence of her sisters and God. Until the day of her death I received a card from her on the anniversary of the retreat reminding me that she was still holding on to that liberating truth.

If we have taken the step which Jesus asks of us – namely making his word our home – we are able to begin our heart-to-heart conversation with God. God has spoken first; he has assured you that you are very special to him. How are you going to respond?

Pause for a moment right now and make your response.

The Holy Spirit inspired this response for our prayer: "It was you who created my inmost self, and put me together in my mother's womb; for all these mysteries I thank you: for the wonder of myself, for the wonder of your works" (Psalm 139:13). Use this response frequently in your prayer.

54

Notice how you feel as you thank God for the wonder of yourself. Don't be surprised if you feel insincere or even incapable of saying the words. This response comes from the deep conviction that God created you with great love. If you haven't got that deep conviction in your heart at this moment you will find it difficult to use these words. You will probably feel much more comfortable saying: "Oh God, be merciful to me a sinner". But it is the same Holy Spirit who inspires both of these responses. And the Holy Spirit, as Paul assures us, is praying in us long before we get round to praying ourselves (Romans 8:26). Not only that, but at the right hand of the Father Jesus is also praying for us. Tom Smail writes: "Not only are we being prayed for by the ascended Son, but we are being prayed in by the indwelling Spirit."[6] If you find it difficult to thank God for the wonder of yourself, then allow the Holy Spirit to pray that prayer in you, and thank God that Jesus is saying that prayer for you in heaven. Then relax in the awareness that both Christ and the Spirit are interceding on your behalf at this very moment.

When you have thanked God for the wonder of yourself, thank God for the wonder of all those in your life, especially those who may be causing you trouble.

Pause for a moment now and do that. Allow the people in your life to come into your mind and heart and thank God for them.

Now notice how you feel as you thank God for the wonder of your enemies. You have to say something to God about your enemies. Since your enemies are precious in God's sight, there would not be much point in trying to turn God against them; nor would it make sense to ask God to change them and make them better people, because that would be sitting in judgement on them. The only thing you can do with regard to your enemies is to act on the words of the Gospel. Jesus tells us to love our enemies and pray for those who persecute us (Matthew 5:44). The most liberating and healing way

---

6 Tom Smail, *The Giving Gift: the Holy Spirit in person* (London: Darton, Longman & Todd, 1994), 208.

to pray for your enemies is to thank God for the wonder of their being. This can be a most challenging prayer. But Christ and the Spirit are interceding for and in them too. Your attempt to thank God for the wonder of their being will indicate clearly whether you have, as yet, fully forgiven them. And as you pray you will receive the grace to forgive. The hurts they have caused you will be healed and they will no longer have power over you.

Acknowledgement

The second step in listening to God and using his word in our prayer is to acknowledge what he is doing in our life. Our Lady shows us the way. She knew how to ponder God's word in her heart. When Elizabeth praised her with the words: "Of all women you are the most blessed" (Luke 1:42), Mary responded: "the Almighty has done great things for me" (verse 49). Elizabeth's praise comes from the Holy Spirit and is what releases the Magnificat in Mary's heart. There is a Magnificat in each human heart and the heart will remain sad until it has sung it. Mary did not refuse Elizabeth's praise. She accepted it and acknowledged that God had done great things for her.

I sometimes do an exercise with a group: everyone makes two columns on a piece of paper. In the left column they write their positive points, and their negative points on the right. Most people find they have no problem filling the right-hand column, but can find very little to put on the left.

If we can't acknowledge the good things God is doing in our life we won't be able to enter into Mary's prayer of praise:

> My soul proclaims the greatness of the Lord
> and my spirit exults in God my saviour;
> because he has looked upon his lowly handmaid.
> Yes, from this day forward all generations will call me blessed,
> for the Almighty has done great things for me.
> Holy is his name (Luke 1:47-49)

The good thing that God was doing in Mary's life led her to proclaim God's greatness, not her own, and to exult in God her saviour, not in herself.

C. S. Lewis said: "praise almost seems to be inner health made audible."[7] Acknowledging with gratitude the good things that God is doing in our lives is not only a sign of inner health, but also the means for achieving inner health. As we pray in the preface of the Mass: "You have no need of our praise, yet our desire to thank you is itself your gift." God gives us the desire to acknowledge and praise him because in this way he makes us whole. When you are feeling peace and joy it can be easy to praise God. But even when you do not feel at peace with God it is still necessary to acknowledge his goodness and praise him. If the cause of the lack of peace is sin then, of course, the first step in prayer is repentance. The great king David prayed:

> Have mercy on me, O God, in your goodness,
> in your great tenderness wipe away my faults;
> wash me clean of my guilt,
> purify me from my sin (Psalm 51:1).

A confident appeal to God's goodness. If our inability to acknowledge the good things that God is doing in our lives is caused by alienation from God, our union with God is restored through the grace of conversion, which implies a profound change of the whole person. King David also asked for something else:

> Instil some joy and gladness into me,
> let the bones you have crushed rejoice again (Psalm 51:8).

David knew the need for praise; he knew how important it was to acknowledge God's goodness. And, therefore, after confessing his sinfulness, he asked for the gift of joy so that he could truly give

---

7 C.S. Lewis, *Reflections on the Psalms* (London: Geoffrey Bles, 1958), 80.

glory to God. As we acknowledge God's goodness we give him glory because we become more fully alive in his presence. His name is hallowed in us.

Sometimes, however, you may experience great dryness in your prayer. You want to pray but feel unable; you want to acknowledge the great things that God is doing but you are unable to identify them; you long for the presence of God but you are only aware of his absence. In those times the only safe rule is to persevere in prayer and wait for the Lord: "I waited patiently for the Lord, he inclined to me and heard my cry" (Psalm 40:1).

Waiting for the Lord, especially in times of darkness, pain or loss, is the essential disposition of the disciple. Sister Bernarde describes this condition:

> I have to say, that the times that have been the richest and most growth-filled in my life were the times I have experienced the cross of darkness, abandonment and loss. This is where, above all, I discovered the truth of who I am and who God was for me. It is from this place of acute pain of a recent bereavement (a close friend for forty years) that I share my thought with you now. In the past weeks, in moments of poignant suffering and desolation the word of God ministered powerfully to me through sometimes very mundane circumstances. God spoke directly and personally through a "Prayer for the Day", a liturgical reading, a scripture quote on a card – words dropping like dew on arid ground bringing meaningful insights... I have learned in the past few weeks the truth of the words "blessed are they who mourn for they shall be comforted"; comforted with the knowledge that they are growing creatively towards still more new life to become a new creation.[8]

---

8 Sister Bernarde, private correspondence, 1996.

Did you ever have the experience of waiting for a friend? A five-minute wait is bearable; an hour can be very trying; a five-hour wait would be almost unbearable. Yet, if you knew your friend was really on the way, you would wait. In the same spirit we have to wait for the Lord, acknowledging what he is doing in our life. And when he comes we will be filled with the spirit of praise and thanksgiving.

Having acknowledged the good things which God is doing in our own life we should then acknowledge what he is doing in the lives of those who are close to us, especially in the lives of our enemies. This keeps us free from the danger of entering into judgement on our enemy: "Do not judge, and you will not be judged; because the judgements you give are the judgements you will get" (Matthew 7:1).

Allowance
The third step in using the word of God in prayer is to make allowance for our own weakness and sinfulness. The only thing we can do when we sin is to ask God's pardon. We cannot forgive our own sins, but we must forgive ourselves for sinning. Self-acceptance means that we accept ourselves as weak and sinful, and that when we fail we should not be devastated. Self-acceptance ensures that we can let go, accept that we have sinned, that God has forgiven us as we repented, and then forgive ourselves. If we don't forgive ourselves we become burdened with guilt, and guilt prevents us from looking God in the eye. Feeling guilty, even after receiving forgiveness, inhibits our prayer as a heart-to-heart conversation with the Lord.

In the presence of God, then, we make allowance for our own weaknesses. Then we make allowance for the weaknesses of others, especially our enemy. After we forgive our enemy, the most liberating thing we can say is that we make allowance for his weaknesses: "Father, forgive them, they do not know what they are doing" (Luke 23:34).

Centring Prayer

Centring prayer is an ancient and traditional form of prayer. It is seeking to be in love in the presence of God – not seeking to do anything or say anything, but simply be in God's presence.

In order to be in God's presence we have to be at the centre of our own being, because that is where God is. God is closer to me than I am to myself; God dwells in the very depths of my being. Centring prayer takes this truth of faith and seeks to dwell with the God who dwells in us. We centre, then, and enter into the depths of our being in faith. And in love and desire we focus on God. The great Archbishop of Canterbury St Anselm gave us this direction for prayer:

> Enter into the inner chamber of your soul, shut out everything save God and what can be of help in your quest for him and having locked the door seek him out. Speak now, my whole heart, speak now to God: I seek your countenance, O Lord, your countenance I seek. Come then, Lord my God, teach my heart where and how to seek you, where and how to find you.[9]

All prayer is God's gift to us before it becomes our prayer, but we have to take steps to be ready to receive the gift. When I introduce groups to centring prayer I make the following points:

- Centring prayer is based on scripture: "Be still, and know that I am God" (Psalm 46:10).
- In order to be still we must first still the body. We do this by sitting upright, both feet firmly on the floor, hands relaxed. Then we breathe rhythmically and deeply and silently; in through the nose and silently exhaling through the mouth.
- After about a minute or two the body becomes still and can remain in that position for a long time.

---

9 Office of Readings, Friday 1st Week of Advent.

- As the body stills, the mind becomes more focused.
- Because we are being still in the presence of God, our stillness is our prayer. We focus on where we are – in God's presence. We do so wordlessly. We say nothing and do nothing; we just remain still in the presence.
- Because we are still in God's presence there will be a "prayer word" – a sacred word in our heart. It may be Jesus, or Lord, or Father, or Holy Spirit, or Mother Mary; it may be a symbol such as water or fire.
- When we find our minds have wandered, we simply say the word in our hearts and we become refocused.
- Distractions are part of the experience of praying. Note that distractions take the mind away to something else. One moment you are still in God's presence, next moment your mind may be in Australia. But you are not in Australia! You stay where you want to be – namely in God's presence.
- Distractions only affect the mind. They do not cancel out your intention to be still in God's presence. It is, therefore, vital that we convince ourselves that we are not our thoughts and distractions, and focus on our desire to be with God.
- Distractions don't make our prayer a waste of time. The essence of prayer consists in our intention to give the time to God and not on our successful performance. Each time we keep our intention to pray, God accepts our intention.
- If prayer is not the priority in our lives then we find ourselves praying "when we have time" or "when we feel like it". If we organise our prayer lives this way we soon find we have less and less time and inclination.
- If prayer is not the priority in our day it will take second place to every other good work or every other mood.

The Word of God in Catholic devotion to Mary the Mother of Jesus[10]

First let us look at how we base our devotion to Mary entirely on the word of God. We begin with some practical steps, using the prayer exercises that you have become familiar with at the end of each chapter of this book.

- Find a quiet place where you can be still. Sit in a comfortable position, with your spine straight, both feet firmly on the floor and breathe deeply and rhythmically.
- As you breathe rhythmically your whole body will begin to relax and the tension will begin to ebb away.
- In faith recognise that you are in the presence of God.
- Listen to the word of Jesus as he says, "This is your mother" (John 19:27). Thank Jesus for this gift of his own mother. Thank him for speaking this word of God and ask him for the grace to live by it.
- Recall that Jesus speaks the word of God to his mother: "This is your son" (John 19:26). Mary is living by that word, and with a motherly heart she is anxious to be close to you. Jesus has entrusted you, through his word from the cross, to his mother. Can you entrust yourself to her?
- Accept these life-giving words of Jesus. Accept that Mary is your spiritual mother.
- Speak to Mary in your heart, with the words of your heart. Or greet her as the Archangel Gabriel and Elizabeth did: "Blessed are you among women, and blessed is the fruit of your womb." You are now seeing Mary through the light of the Gospel. Your attitude to her is being formed by the word of the Gospel; you are fulfilling her own prophecy and calling her blessed.
- Having acknowledged Mary for who she really is, you may want to ask for her prayers. The Church has said

---

10 For a more detailed study of Mary's place in the life and spirituality of the Christian, see my book, *All Generations Will Call Me Blessed* (Chawton: Redemptorist Publications, 2007).

this prayer, the second part of the Hail Mary, for many centuries: "Holy Mary, Mother of God, pray for us sinners now and at the hour of our death." The Church teaches us to honour Mary as holy, while presenting ourselves as sinners in the sure knowledge that she, like her son, loves sinners.

- You are now in a devotional relationship with Mary. The Holy Spirit will fill your heart with love for her. That love will find its own expression. Your personal devotion to Mary may be very different from that of others. Your devotion is a gift of love given to you by the Holy Spirit. With that love in your heart you begin to live by the word of God: "This is your mother."

- As you become aware of the gift of the Mother of God as your own mother, aware of her love and presence in your life, you will find that your heart will want to say something else to Mary. It will be entirely personal to you. St Aloysius Gonzaga used to repeat with holy amazement, "Mother of God and my mother". Meditation on those simple words will lead you very deep into a faith relationship with Mary.

- As you begin to pray the Hail Mary you will become aware of so many truths: "The Lord is with you" (Luke 1:29), the angel proclaims that God the Father is with Mary. The Father is with Mary in such a loving, personal way that he invites her, with divine courtesy, to agree to the great miracle of the incarnation. Meditating on God the Father's request to his lowly handmaid is always fruitful. The Father had such regard for Mary that he sent the Archangel Gabriel to her to ask her consent. He didn't command; he invited.

- The angel told Mary that she would conceive by the power of the Holy Spirit: "The Holy Spirit will come upon you... and the power of the Most High will cover you with its shadow" (verse 35). At the beginning of the Book of Genesis we are told that God's Spirit "hovered over the water" (1:2). God's Spirit will hover over Mary, if she agrees, and there will be a new creation.

- Mary responds: "Let what you have said be done to me" (Luke 1:38), and the great miracle of the incarnation takes place. She becomes, through the power of the Spirit, the Mother of God. She is truly the temple of the Holy Spirit, the dwelling place of God.

- Devotion to Mary always leads to a contemplation of the mystery of the Father, Son and Holy Spirit. We are led to contemplate what the Holy Trinity did in Mary. The Father chose her and requested her consent; the Holy Spirit overshadowed her; the Son became incarnate in her womb. All the beauty we admire and revere in her is a reflection of what the Holy Trinity did in her. She is Holy Mary because God the Father is with her; she is the virgin mother because the Holy Spirit overshadowed her; she is the mother of our salvation because Jesus Christ was born of her.

- Once we begin to meditate on Mary and her relationship with Jesus, we find ourselves meditating on the mysteries of the life of Jesus: his conception, birth, childhood, public life, passion, death, resurrection, ascension and outpouring of the Holy Spirit. As we take his words from the cross: "This is your mother", and ponder them in our hearts, we are gently led into the contemplation of the mystery of the Holy Trinity and our own salvation.

Personal spiritual exercise

- Centre yourself, using the techniques we have just outlined.
- Bring yourself to bodily stillness and calm.
- Now ask yourself, what intention do I have in my heart about giving time to God in prayer?
- Be still and listen.
- Now focus again on your breathing.
- And bring yourself gently back to the world.

5

Abba, Father

A missionary sister writes from Ecuador:

> Like many people of my generation – nearing sixty – I grew up with a stern father, and an image of God the Father as very strict – demanding perfection from me all the time, with that infamous "big book" ready to jot down my failures. Obviously, I failed in my religious life. Nobody could live up to what I thought was expected of me. So I left, and tried to find happiness in possessions and addictions. God my Father waited patiently, lovingly and through many failures and mistakes, he drew me back to himself. During a retreat before coming out here the true image of God my loving father was revealed to me and I'm still discovering the wonders of his goodness. I am now working in a slum area of Ecuador trying to help his poor children. I brought back a plaque from Kinnoull.[1] "I will never forget you, I have carved you on the palm of my hands," and it hangs on my wall as

---

1 St Mary's, The Redemptorist Centre of Spirituality, where this Sister was doing her sabbatical programme is located at Kinnoull, a district of the city of Perth in Scotland.

a constant reminder. The one phrase I carried away from Kinnoull… is that I am precious in his eyes.

When this sister's image of God was that of a stern father, demanding perfection, she didn't have the strength and joy to live her life as a religious. Her religious practice was joyless. When, however, the true image of God her loving Father was revealed to her, she found joy and fulfilment in doing the loving Father's will in serving the poor. There is a great lesson in this. What is our image of God? How do we approach God in our daily life?

Thinking about God is not always the most helpful way to approach the mystery of the divine. Other forms of human activity – such as yearning, longing, seeking, thirsting and desiring – enable us to enter more fully into the mystery. While thinking strives for clear ideas, the longing or yearning of the heart seeks a relationship. It is the heart and not the mind that reaches out, in the first place, to God. As Elizabeth Johnson observes:

> The living God literally cannot be compared with anything in the world. To do so is to reduce divine reality to an idol. This divine magnitude means that no matter how much we know, the human mind can never capture the whole of the living God in a net of concepts, images, or definitions, or preside over the reality of God in even the most exalted doctrines. A Zen-like riddle preached by Augustine preserves this wisdom succinctly: "If you have understood, it is not God" (Sermon 117.5). If you have fully figured out who God is, then you are dealing with something else, some lesser reality. It is a matter of the livingness of God, who is not just a bigger and better object in the world, but unspeakably Other.[2]

We can only approach the mystery of the divine by way of images and metaphors. The universe and everything within it give us a glimpse of God, because ultimately everything comes from God –

---

2 Elizabeth Johnson, *Quest for the Living God: Mapping Frontiers in the Theology of God* (New York: Continuum, 2007), 13.

but the glimpse is not God. We can say, "Look, God is like this", or "God is as close as that", or "God is love". But no human word or image can define God, because God is, by definition, infinite. And that can be a very hard concept to struggle with.

Years ago I was having a long conversation with a young political activist in Northern Ireland. She was a brilliant student, deeply involved in the civil rights movement. She said she no longer believed in God. When she described in detail the god she didn't believe in I shocked her by saying that I didn't believe in the god she had rejected either. While her political philosophy was very advanced, her theological concept hadn't changed from childhood. Instead of finding God within her passion for social justice and human rights, she was rejecting the god out there, that old man with the white beard thundering dos and don'ts from on high, who didn't seem to be bothered about injustice. I suggested that if she entered into the heart of her passion for justice and truth, she would begin to encounter the God that her hero Martin Luther King knew. The God of justice needs the human passion for justice in a world where human freedom is so often used in the cause of injustice and oppression. I was encouraging her to ask herself this very basic question: where does her passion for justice come from?

The God question

How do we approach God? Through our intellect, seeking scientific clarity, or through our hearts, seeking human fulfilment? Clearly there should be no conflict between these approaches, but in things of the spirit, in that world of deep human yearning and longing, the heart knows more than the head. In the words of French philosopher Blaise Pascal, "the heart has its reasons which reason knows nothing of."[3]

Karl Rahner loved to argue that the biggest logical problem in most arguments against atheism was a very inadequate theism, a

---

3 Blaise Pascal, *Pensées* (Penguin Classics Revised Ed.) (London: Penguin, 2003), 127.

poor theology.[4] Rahner invited people to enter into their hearts, to discover the immense world within, and as they entered their own inner world they would begin to discover the presence of the living God. The yearning of the heart is not for clear ideas but for loving relationship. To reduce theology to ideas, or talk about God's existence or non-existence, is to ignore the deep heart and give priority to abstract thoughts.

Relationship, not ideas; yearning and seeking, not thinking and defining; longing to belong, not defining to clarify! The way of the heart is different from the way of the head. And, in our search for the presence of God, we follow the way of the heart. What is that deep, restless yearning in the human heart? Where does it come from? What can satisfy it? After a long struggle to identify the nature of that yearning St Augustine burst forth with his memorable words:

> Too late have I loved you, O Beauty so ancient and so new, too late have I loved you! Behold, you were within me, while I was outside; it was there I sought you, and, a deformed creature, rushed headlong upon these things of beauty which you have made. You were with me, but I was not with you. They kept me far from you, those fair things which, if they were not in you, would not exist at all. You have called to me, and have cried out, and have shattered my deafness. You blazed forth with light, and have shone upon me, and you have put blindness to flight! You have sent forth fragrance, and I have drawn my breath, and I pant after you. I have tasted you, and I hunger and thirst after you. You have touched me, and I have burned for your peace.[5]

Our inner world

The serious search for meaning in life, for ultimate values, for God, begins in earnest when we enter into the inner world of our own life

---

4 Johnson, *Quest for the Living God*, 30.

5 St Augustine, *Confessions*, 10, 27.

and experience. It is within the experience of our life that we begin to find signs, or catch glimpses, of the presence of God. We know our heart's capacity for love even in the face of hatred or rejection; we have experienced the presence of hope despite everything that may be going wrong; and even in the midst of the deepest confusion and apparent pointlessness our heart still searches for meaning and purpose. We know the indomitable power within us to survive. And, sooner or later we all ask ourselves the question, "Where does this inner power come from?" or "Who gave me this inner strength?" We are now asking the "God question".

Believers, of course, may think that they find God naturally. But when they meet disaster, or when life seems to be touched by evil, the God they found naturally within can vanish – and they are left with a sense of emptiness and meaninglessness. And we hear the desperate cry, "Where was God when we most needed him?" We have to face the challenge of suffering and say to ourselves, "If the God I believe in, when life is comfortable and going well, cannot be found when things are going badly, then I am not finding the true God of the Bible as revealed by Jesus Christ." For the believer this can be a very uncomfortable statement. We believe in the goodness of God. God is "The Lord, the giver of life". But how can we reconcile the existence of this God with the terrible things that happen in our world?

Our need for revelation

Jesus came to change our image of God. It is good to remind ourselves that God is total mystery, total silence, and we would have known very little about him if he hadn't broken the silence. That's what we mean by revelation – God breaking the silence. And God breaks the silence in the same way as we break the silence about ourselves – God spoke. As scripture says:

> At various times in the past and in various different ways, God spoke to our ancestors through the prophets; but in our own time, the last days, he has spoken to us through his

Son, the Son that he has appointed to inherit everything and through whom he made everything there is (Hebrews 1:1-2).

We would have known very little about God if God hadn't spoken. Yet the desire for God is written in the human heart. Because of this desire the human heart is always searching. As St Augustine puts it: "You have made us for yourself, O Lord, and our hearts will find no rest until they rest in you."[6] The Church has always taught that we can acknowledge God's existence through observing the world which exists. St Paul said:

> For what can be known about God is perfectly plain to them since God himself has made it plain. Ever since God created the world his everlasting power and deity – however invisible – have been there for the mind to see in the things he has made (Romans 1:19-20).

The human heart's desire for God has led people in every age to search for God. As the Catechism says:

> In many ways, throughout history down to the present day, men have given expression to their quest for God in their religious beliefs and behaviour: in prayers, sacrifices, rituals, meditations and so forth. These forms of religious expression, despite the ambiguities they often bring with them, are so universal that one may well call man a religious being.[7]

God does not leave us, however, to the power of our own intellects. He wants to make himself known to us. That personal knowledge of God is promised in the new covenant. Jesus sums up his work in terms of making God's name known: "I have given them the teaching you gave to me and they have truly accepted this, that I came from you, and have believed that it was you who sent me" (John 17:8).

---

6 St Augustine, *Confessions*, 1, 1.

7 *Catechism of the Catholic Church*, 14, 28.

When his disciples have accepted all this, Jesus is able to say to God: "I have… finished the work that you gave me to do" (John 17:4). He sees his work on earth completed because he has revealed God's name to his disciples and they have accepted it. And the name Jesus gave to God is Abba, loving Father.

The Word incarnate

We can come to the knowledge of God's existence through the light of our own reason; we could never know the intimate nature of God, or understand our own relationship with God, without a direct revelation. To communicate directly with us, God had to do two things simultaneously: he had to speak a word which we could understand, and he had to speak a word which, at the same time, would truly manifest his inner being. As the scripture says: "In the beginning was the Word: the Word was with God and the Word was God" (John 1:1).

Jesus, the word incarnate, speaks the infinite word to us in our own human words. And he tells us that the one he calls his Father is also our Father. That is what we mean by revelation. God in his own inner nature is total silence. In breaking the silence, through the Word made flesh, we receive the knowledge that God, the source of all power, the maker of heaven and earth, does not want to be known by his omnipotence, his infinitude, his absolute perfection. God wants to be known by a name which is in the heart of every child: the name Father.

In teaching us to pray Jesus did not tell us to say almighty, everlasting, eternal and infinite divine One. He told us to say Abba, Father. It was as if he said: "If you want to come to God you must come with the sentiment of a child in your heart and the word of a child on your lips." We do not try to figure God out with our minds, rather we go out to God with our hearts and love him as our Father.

A name expresses a person's essence and identity and the meaning of the person's life. God has a name; he is not an anonymous force. To disclose one's name is to make oneself known to others; in a way it is to hand oneself over by becoming accessible, capable of being known more intimately and addressed personally.[8]

Jesus makes God totally accessible by teaching us to address God, the creator of all, as Abba, loving Father. He opens up to us the possibility of getting to know God in an entirely new way – in an intimate, personal, loving way. What could give us greater joy than the knowledge that God is our Father and that we are his sons and daughters?

The image of the father expresses God's loving care and goodness. But could we also use the image of the mother to speak about God? The Catechism of the Catholic Church states:

> By calling God "Father", the language of faith indicates two things: that God is first origin of everything and transcendent authority; and that he is at the same time goodness and loving care for all his children. God's parental tenderness can also be expressed by the image of motherhood, which emphasises God's immanence, the intimacy between Creator and creature.[9]

If the image of father doesn't speak to you about the goodness and love of God, the image of mother may do so. In the scriptures, God compares himself to a mother: "At her breast will her nurselings be carried and fondled in her lap. Like a son comforted by his mother will I comfort you" (Isaiah 66:13). And in the Psalms we read: "Enough for me to keep my soul tranquil and quiet like a child in its mother's arms, as content as a child that has been weaned" (131:2).

Jesus, in revealing God to us as our Father, calls us into an intimate, trusting, loving relationship with our heavenly Father. But

---

8   *Catechism of the Catholic Church*, 50, 203.

9   As above, 57, 239.

not everyone finds the image of father comforting. Pope Benedict XVI, speaking about the Lord's Prayer, writes:

> It is true, of course, that contemporary men and women have difficulty experiencing the great consolation of the word father immediately, since the experience of the father is in many cases either completely absent or is obscured by inadequate examples of fatherhood.[10]

There can be a "father wound" in the heart, a space left empty because of the absence of one's father – the absence of a father's loving presence and care. But that wound can be healed when it is brought to the Lord. Indeed Jesus described his own ministry as one of binding up the broken heart.

Proof that we are sons and daughters

In the Mass as we prepare for the Lord's prayer, we say: "Jesus has taught us to call God our Father and so we have the courage to say, Our Father…". We can call God "Father" because he has given us the greatest possible proof that we are his children. In his Letter to the Romans, St Paul says: "The Spirit himself and our spirit bear united witness that we are children of God" (8:16). It is not just the teaching of Jesus which enables us to say "Father"; it is the Spirit of Jesus within us and united to us, which makes us truly sons and daughters of the Father. Through the transforming action of the Spirit we are made one with Christ, divinised. As we pray in the Mass: "By the mystery of this water and wine may we come to share in the divinity of Christ, who humbled himself to share in our humanity." This divinisation takes place through the sanctifying and transforming presence of the Holy Spirit.

Writing in the fifth century, St Gregory Nazianzen said: "Acknowledge that you have been made a son of God, a co-heir with Christ. Acknowledge, and now I speak with daring, that you have been made divine. From where and from whom have all these

---

10 Pope Benedict, *Jesus of Nazareth*, 135.

benefits come to you?"[11] Having transformed us into the children of God the Spirit then teaches us how to pray. He cries out, "Abba, Father". That is our new relationship with God. St Ignatius of Antioch, one of the great early martyrs wrote: "I feel a spring of living water within me murmuring: come to the Father."[12]

This revelation that the almighty God is our loving Father transforms our attitude and approach in prayer. After they had sinned, our first parents lost confidence in God's abiding, fatherly love and hid (Genesis 3:8). Fear and distrust had entered their lives. Their vision of God had changed. Ever since then, God has been trying to convince us that he loves us, that he is on our side and wants to save us from our sins and unite us to himself for ever. Jesus called this desire in the heart of God "the Gospel" – the good news. And he taught us to acknowledge this with one simple word: Abba. That says it all. When we address God as Abba we not only profess our faith in the Gospel preached by Jesus, we also acknowledge that through his death and resurrection we have become children of God. As St John said: "Think of the love that the Father has lavished on us, by letting us be called God's children; and that is what we are" (1 John 3:1).

The reaction of children at the sight of their father teaches us how to pray. As soon as children see their father returning from work they run to meet him. So often we treat God as if he were a stranger, as if we didn't really know him. Jesus has revealed the Father to us. This revelation is the source of our joy and peace because now we come to God not as a stern father but as our loving Abba.

Pause for a moment now and ask Jesus to reveal the Father to you. Listen to the voice of the Spirit within crying Abba, Father.

---

11 Office of Readings, Monday 1st Week of Lent.

12 Office of Readings, Tuesday Week 10.

Angela's testimony

The following testimony expresses in terms of a woman's own experience of God her Father much of what I am trying to say in this chapter:

> Although I knew that my Father loved me very much, circumstances being as they were, I was not able to experience that love. Even as a tiny child I had a strong sense of God, and a close relationship with Jesus, but I never knew God as my Father, or had any personal relationship with him. Then, one day, Jesus took me to his Father. I was at a large gathering of people singing hymns of praise and worship. Suddenly, I felt myself to be in the presence of God in a very intimate way. I knew him to be my Father, and I his child, and that he loved me dearly. I put my arms around him, asking him with all my heart, that my life would be pleasing to him, and that I would fulfil his plan for me. Since that day, I have known God as a tender and loving Father. He cares about the little details of my life, and I am aware of his provision and protection in very ordinary circumstances. Sometimes I experience myself in his arms, and there is a security I have never known before. I understand now the meaning of a Father's love, a tender forgiving love, and that he has hopes and plans for my life (as a human father would). I come to him often as a Father, and speak to him about myself and others. He always listens and understands, and prayers are answered in many unexpected ways. Sometimes I feel the tender love he has for his children, and the longing of his heart that all may know him as their Father. I pray that my life will give him glory and honour and that I will bring others to know him.

Angela's testimony highlights two important facts. Firstly, Jesus brought her to the Father. Jesus himself said: "No one can come to the Father except through me" (John 14:6). Secondly, in her first personal experience of God as her loving Father, she asked that her life might be pleasing to him. She said, in effect, "Hallowed be thy name". It is a good indicator that this was an authentic religious experience. This experience is still bearing fruit in her life. She has become an intercessor for all God's people. Only those who know the goodness, the kindness and the mercy of the Father can give themselves wholeheartedly to the prayer of intercession.

Personal spiritual exercise

- Centre yourself, using the techniques we learned in week one.
- Bring yourself to bodily stillness and calm.
- Reflect on your relationship with God. Do you come to God as a loving Father or Mother?
- Now ask yourself: Do I really want Jesus to reveal God to me?
- Accept yourself just as you are in the presence of your Father.
- Now focus again on your breathing.
- And bring yourself gently back to the world.

6

Jesus Christ is Lord

The first proclamation of our Christian faith found in the New Testament is enshrined in the words "Jesus Christ is Lord". This proclamation, like the assurance that we are sons and daughters of the Father, is the work of the Holy Spirit. Paul tells us that: "no one can say 'Jesus is Lord' unless he is under the influence of the Holy Spirit" (1 Corinthians 12:3). Peter, on the first Pentecost Sunday, proclaimed to the people of Jerusalem: "The whole House of Israel can be certain that God has made this Jesus whom you crucified both Lord and Christ" (Acts 2:36).

Jesus Christ is Lord. We will consider each of these holy names. Cardinal Congar OP wrote that in the Middle Ages the scholastic theologians regarded "Christ" as simply a proper noun or name that could be replaced equally well by "Jesus" or "the Lord".[1] If theologians have confused the holy names in this way, it's hardly surprising if many people speak of Jesus Christ in much the way they would speak of John Smith. But whereas Smith is a family name, Christ is not. Indeed, we do not know the Holy Family's name.

---

1   Yves Congar, *I Believe in the Holy Spirit vol.1* (London: Chapman, 1983), 23.

It was only when I began to reflect on the role of the Holy Spirit in the life of Jesus that I began to see that Christ is not a surname and Lord is not an honorary title. Jesus is Christ and he is Lord, because of the work of the Spirit.

Jesus

In the Hebrew language Jesus means "God saves". Right from the start, it was made very clear to Mary and Joseph what their son was to be named:

> Listen! You are to conceive a son, and you must name him Jesus. He will be great and will be called the Son of the Most High (Luke 1:32).

> Joseph son of David, do not be afraid to take Mary home as your wife, because she has conceived what is in her by the Holy Spirit. She will give birth to a son and you must name him Jesus, because he is the one who is to save his people from their sins (Matthew 1:21).

Every time in our prayer when we say the name Jesus we are in effect saying: "You are the one who saves us from our sins". God alone can forgive sins, so when we acknowledge that Jesus saves us from our sins we are professing our faith in his divinity. The Catechism puts it this way:

> The name Jesus signifies that the very name of God is present in the person of his Son, made man for the universal and definitive redemption from sins. It is the divine name that alone brings salvation, and henceforth all can invoke his name, for Jesus united himself to all men through his incarnation, so that there is no other name under heaven given among men by which we must be saved.[2]

---

2 *Catechism of the Catholic Church*, 96, 432.

Paul discovered this for himself in a very dramatic way on the Road to Damascus:

> Suddenly, while he was travelling to Damascus and just before he reached the city, there came a light from heaven all round him. He fell to the ground, and then he heard a voice saying, "Saul, Saul, why are you persecuting me?" "Who are you, Lord?" he asked, and the voice answered, "I am Jesus, and you are persecuting me" (Acts 9:3-6).

Hearing the name Jesus uttered from the light transformed him from Saul, a persecutor of Christians, into the great St Paul. And the name of Jesus took on a whole new dimension for him after that:

> But God raised him high
> and gave him the name
> which is above all other names
> so that all beings
> in the heavens, on earth and in the underworld,
> should bend the knee at the name of Jesus
> and that every tongue should acclaim
> Jesus Christ as Lord,
> to the glory of God the Father (Philippians 2:9-11).

Coming to believe in Jesus is always accompanied with great reverence for his holy name. It is by the name of Jesus that we are saved, as Peter told the Jews: "For of all the names in the world given to men, this is the only one by which we can be saved" (Acts 4:12). Jesus also assures us: "For where two or three meet in my name, I shall be there with them" (Matthew 18:20). It is why the name of Jesus is at the centre of our prayer, and indeed, we conclude all our prayers in the Mass with the formula: "through our Lord Jesus Christ, your Son."

Just to repeat the name in our hearts is to pray in a most fruitful way. The great saints and mystics of the Eastern Church have developed the Jesus Prayer, which involves repeating the words: "Lord Jesus Christ, Son of God, have mercy on me, a sinner." By repeating this prayer with love and devotion it suddenly, as it were, leaves the head and becomes embedded in the heart, so that, even when the head is busy about other things, the heart still repeats the prayer.

Some years ago I was in the Benedictine monastery at Pecos, where the monks are taught great respect for the holy Name, and repeat it over and again in their prayers. I found that the experience brought great peace into my heart. Even if our only prayer in a whole day is the reverential utterance of the name of Jesus, we have prayed well.

We're told that at the name of Jesus every knee should bow (Philippians 2:10). Pause for a moment now and reflect on your reverence for the name of Jesus. Now repeat it prayerfully in your heart. Or, if you prefer use the Jesus Prayer: "Lord Jesus Christ, Son of God, have mercy on me, a sinner."

Taking the holy name of Jesus in vain is endemic in our society, even among Christians. But it is rarely, if ever, a deliberate insult or blasphemy. I have often heard very good people exclaim "O Jesus Christ!" or "Christ almighty!" I once, at an airport, saw a harassed woman with three young children. When the last call for the flight to Dublin was announced, she exclaimed "O Jesus, Mary and Joseph, we're late!" Everyone burst out laughing as the three children (not Jesus, Mary and Joseph) began to run for the departure gate.

But this bad habit can be stopped more easily if we're aware what we're really saying. It is actually a very good practice each time you hear the Holy Name used in vain, to give it its due reverence in your own heart. When someone exclaims, "O Jesus Christ!" turn it into a profession of faith by saying in your heart, "You are Lord", or

"You are risen from the dead", or "You are now with us". You will be surprised to discover how often an apparent blasphemy turns your heart to prayer. But be careful not to sit in judgement on whoever said it in the first place.

Christ

The word "Christ" comes from the Greek translation of the Hebrew word *Messiah*, which means "anointed". So Christ means "the anointed one". As Raniero Cantalamessa points out, the Early Fathers made the link between Jesus' anointing when the Holy Spirit descended on him after his Baptism in the form of a dove, and his becoming the Christ, or Messiah:

> According to some of them, just as at the incarnation, the Word had become "Jesus", so at his baptismal anointing he had become "Christ", that is to say God's Anointed One, the Messiah. As they saw it, the mystery of the anointing was so important that the very name "Christians" was derived from it: "This is why we are called Christians (*christianoi*)," writes one of them, "because we are anointed (*chriometha*) with the oil of God". Christians, according to this explanation, did not so much mean "followers of Christ", as the pagans at Antioch who had been the first to call them this intended... but rather "sharers in Christ's anointing".[3]

Thus the name Jesus Christ can be substituted with the expression "Jesus, the Anointed One". St Basil wrote: "To name Christ is to confess the whole Trinity, because it indicates the God who anointed, and the Son who was anointed, and that wherewith he was anointed, namely the Spirit."[4]

In this sense the Church is the community of those who share in the anointing of Jesus. In baptism we are baptised "in Christ", as

---

3 R. Cantalamessa, *The Holy Spirit in the Life of Jesus* (Collegeville Minnesota: The Liturgical Press, 1994), 6.

4 As above, 7.

Paul put it (Romans 6:3). We come to share in what makes Jesus "the Christ" – namely the anointing of the Holy Spirit. In other words we become "Christ-ed", anointed ones, Christs ourselves. When we ask someone their Christian name we are asking what name they received when they were joined to Christ. Our Christian name is given to the new creation which we became when we are christened. Guardini writes:

> The person himself is changed by this daily contact with Christ, becoming more and more similar to his model. The believer remains in his profession; he remains the same trader, postman, doctor that he was, with the same duties. The machine does not function better in his hand than in that of another; the diagnosis is not easier than it was, yet work performed in Christ is somehow different. No longer overestimated, but properly evaluated, it assumes a new dignity and earnestness; is performed with a new conscientiousness. The same holds true for worries and pain and all other human need. The difference is indefinable, visible only in the result: here an illness or loss borne with quiet heroism, there an old enmity healed. In Christ all things are changed.[5]

Pause for a moment now. Envisage the Holy Spirit coming on Jesus and anointing him; then see Jesus sharing that anointing with you. And with St Peter say to Jesus: "You are the Christ, the Son of the living God."

Devotion to Christ as the Anointed One is beautifully expressed in the prayer known as St Patrick's Breastplate:

> Christ be with me, Christ within me
> Christ behind me, Christ before me
> Christ beside me, Christ to win me
> Christ to comfort and restore me

---

5 Romano Guardini, *The Lord* (London: Longmans Green & Co., 1954), 446.

Christ beneath me, Christ above me
Christ in quiet, Christ in danger
Christ in hearts of all that love me
Christ in mouth of friend and stranger

Pope Benedict XVI writes:

> The effort to express the mystery of Jesus in titles that explained his mission, indeed, his essence, continued after Easter. Increasingly, three fundamental titles began to emerge: "Christ" (Messiah), "Kyrios" (Lord) and "Son of God". The first title (Christ) taken by itself, made little sense outside of Semitic culture. It quickly ceased to function as a title and was joined with the name of Jesus: Jesus Christ. What began as an interpretation ended up as a name, and therein lies a deeper message. He is completely one with his office; his task and his person are totally inseparable from each other. It was right for this task to become part of his name.[6]

This brings a new nuance to the discussion. Jesus came to fulfil a mission, but it wasn't just to do the work of the Messiah – it was to *be* the Messiah. And so, when we say in our Creed, "We believe in Jesus Christ, his only Son..." we are giving our Saviour his full name, not as a surname, but in recognition of his mission.

Lord

In the Apostles' Creed we say: "I believe in Jesus Christ his only Son, our Lord". Our proclamation of faith is: Jesus Christ is Lord. The title Lord is not interchangeable with the title Christ, nor is it interchangeable with the name of Jesus. We are saying something very specific about Jesus when we say he is "the Christ". We are saying that God his Father has anointed him with the Holy Spirit. What are we saying when we profess that Jesus is Lord? The Gospel puts it this way:

---

6 Pope Benedict, *Jesus of Nazareth*, 319.

> When they saw him they fell down before him, though some hesitated. Jesus came up and spoke to them. He said, "All authority in heaven and on earth has been given to me" (Matthew 28:17-18).

God alone holds all authority in heaven and earth. Jesus is now saying that all that divine authority has been given to him. From heaven Jesus, in our humanity, now exercises that authority. St Mark paints this picture:

> And so the Lord Jesus, after he had spoken to them, was taken up into heaven: there at the right hand of God he took his place, while they, going out, preached everywhere, the Lord working with them and confirming the word by the signs that accompanied it (Mark 16:20).

The apostles had lived and worked with Jesus for about three years. They had got to know him very well. They had listened to his teaching; they had observed his life of prayer and service; they saw the miracles he worked to heal the sick and cast out evil spirits; they were encouraged by his love and support and very proud that he called them his friends. But their world fell apart when he was arrested. One of them had betrayed him, another had denied him, and the rest of them fled. They were devastated by his cruel crucifixion. Yet, within a few days they were back together, proclaiming to the Jews. In the words of Peter: "The whole House of Israel can be certain that God had made this Jesus whom you crucified both Lord and Christ" (Acts 2:36).

The cause of the disciples' devastation, the crucifixion, has become the central message of their proclamation, and they now have a completely new relationship with Jesus. As Peter said to the chief priests and rulers: "This is the stone rejected by you the builders, but which has proved to be the keystone" (Acts 4:11). Jesus is not just their friend and master; nor merely the Messiah promised through the prophets. He is something more. St Thomas, who doubted the story that he had risen from the dead, when he saw him with his own eyes, put it into words: "My Lord and my God!" (John 20:28). The man they had walked the roads of Galilee with, who grew tired and exhausted just as they did, who liked to eat and drink just as they did, was all the time the Son of the Living God. Jesus' resurrection introduced a whole new and totally unexpected dimension to their relationship with him: the dimension of faith.

Jesus underlined this new faith dimension when he said to Thomas: "You believe because you can see me. Happy are those who have not seen and yet believe" (John 20:29). Paul stressed this new faith way of knowing Christ: "Even if we did once know Christ in the flesh, that is not how we know him now" (2 Corinthians 5:16). We know him now through faith. We cannot know Christ in the flesh, or see him with our physical eyes. But we now know through faith that he is sitting at the right hand of the Father.

Having known Jesus in the flesh the disciples now know him in an entirely new way – they know the lordship of Jesus. In the book of Revelation the language takes a very colourful form. John had a vision of the Lord while on the island of Patmos:

> When I saw him, I fell in a dead faint at his feet, but he touched me with his right hand and said, "Do not be afraid; it is I, the First and the Last; I am the Living One. I was dead and now I am to live for ever and ever, and I hold the keys of death and the underworld" (Revelation 1:17-18).

The Lord tells John to write to the angels of the seven churches of Asia with a message. In each message his sovereignty is proclaimed. With these powerful images scripture makes it clear that Jesus now lives in the power and the glory of God. He is King of Kings and Lord of Lords. Faith in his divinity and lordship forced the disciples to re-think not only their personal relationship with him, but also his relationship with the whole of creation. Christ's relationship with the whole of the universe – his cosmic relationship – is expressed in a hymn in the letter to the Colossians:

> He is the image of the unseen God
> and the first-born of all creation,
> for in him were created
> all things in heaven and on earth:
> everything visible and everything invisible,
> Thrones, Dominations, Sovereignties, Powers –
> all things were created through him and for him
> (Colossians 1:15-16).

As Lord, Jesus is not only the head of all creation – all creation was created through him and for him. Everything belongs to him. In a special way we ourselves belong to him. As Paul said: "If we live, we live for the Lord; and if we die, we die for the Lord, so that alive or dead we belong to the Lord" (Romans 14:7). Because we belong to the Lord we have an ever-present source of joy in the Lord, so Paul can say: "I want you to be happy, always happy in the Lord" (Philippians 4:4). If we believe in our hearts that we do belong to the Lord, that he is our Lord and Saviour, then we should resist giving in to passing moods that can darken our spirits. As adults we should gratefully acknowledge our belonging to the Lord, welcome the joy that this belonging brings, and make a formal commitment of our whole lives to him. We can make this commitment in our own words. Some people often find this form of words helpful:

> Lord Jesus Christ, I accept you as my personal Saviour. I am sorry for my sins and ask your forgiveness. I invite you to reign in my heart as Lord. I ask you to fill me and baptise me in your Holy Spirit. I ask you to direct and govern my life and place me where you want me to serve you in your Church under the guidance of your shepherds.

In the next chapter we will consider some of the implications of this commitment.

Take time now to make your own personal commitment to Jesus your Lord. Ask him to come into your life in a new way.

What does it mean to live under the lordship of Jesus? Michelle Moran, a married woman, well-known evangelist and leader of Sion Community, tells us how, after a brief dalliance with a sect based on an Eastern religion, she came to live for the Lord through her involvement with a very committed group of people. They taught her to pray and read the scriptures and she developed a deep love for the Eucharist. She says it's thanks to group leaders, who invested time in her personal development, that she became an informed and involved Roman Catholic. She and her husband were members of a large central London prayer group, and Michelle gradually came to realise that she might have something to offer as a teacher. She says: "Although I didn't realise it at the time, all this was gradually preparing me and laying the foundation for the next step on my journey of faith."

She then recounts how a priest, Fr Pat Lynch, suggested setting up a group of priests, religious and lay people who would travel around the country helping parishes to develop and grow in their mission. Although she listened attentively, it never occurred to her for a minute that she and her husband would be called into such work. However, things changed radically within a matter of months:

> We sold our house… and both of us had given up our jobs in order to work "full time" in the Church. I don't think that God called us because we were extra-ordinary in any way. On the contrary, the fact that we seemed to be "ordinary people" was one of the things which others found attractive. Although both of us had some religious education and formation, neither of us would say that we were theologians or even particularly well versed in the scriptures or Church teaching. However, God used us powerfully in the proclamation of the Gospel and we were able to witness to the love of Christ as we experienced it through our marriage.

It is thirteen years since Michelle wrote this testimony, and the Sion Community is still flourishing and evangelising in Britain and Ireland.[7] But Michelle understands that God still has so much more in store for her:

> As I grow older, I am becoming more and more aware of the fact that conversion is an ongoing process in our lives… I had publicly declared that Jesus was Lord and that my life was now under "new management" but I guess I'll spend the rest of my days learning to submit to that lordship.[8]

Michelle's testimony reveals how Jesus works in the lives of a married couple who come under his lordship. She makes it very clear that when we accept Jesus as Lord, he is free to do new things – even surprising things – in us. And, in the Church today, through the Sion Community and many similar lay-led communities, the Lord is truly doing great things. That is why we must always praise him for the new labourers who are now at work in the vineyard.

Personal spiritual exercise
- Centre yourself, using the techniques we learned in week one.
- Bring yourself to bodily stillness and calm.
- Reflect on your relationship with Jesus. Do you accept him as your Lord? Do you want to accept him as your Lord?
- Invite Jesus to enter your heart as Lord and baptise you in the Holy Spirit.
- Now focus again on your breathing.
- And bring yourself gently back to the world.

---

7 See www.sioncommunity.org.uk

8 Michelle Moran, private correspondence, 1996.

7

Jesus the Lord sends us the Holy Spirit

God's great promise to us is summed up in the words:

> I will pour out my spirit on all mankind.
> Your sons and your daughters shall prophesy,
> your old men shall dream dreams,
> and your young men see visions (Joel 3:1).

The whole of the Bible is the history of how God fulfilled that promise, from his first utterance of the promise until its final fulfilment when God says, "Now I am making the whole of creation new" (Revelation 21:5). In this chapter we will look more directly at the person of the promise – the person of the Holy Spirit.

In the Creed our first profession of faith is that we believe "in the Holy Spirit, the Lord the giver of life. The Holy Spirit is not just a good influence, nor even just the good influence of Jesus. The Holy Spirit is a divine person, equal to the Father and the Son. And, as we say: "With the Father and the Son he is worshipped and glorified". Because the Spirit is a person we can have a personal relationship with him. As Jesus promised: "You know him, because he is with you, he is in you" (John 14:17). We can listen to the Holy Spirit, speak with him, follow his guidance, receive his gifts. Most of all, we can receive the gift of the very presence of the Holy Spirit in our hearts and souls. In the Divine Office we use an ancient hymn which expresses the desire of the Christian heart to be filled with the Spirit:

> Come, Holy Ghost, Creator come
> From thy bright heavenly throne,
> Come, take possession of our souls,
> and make them all thy own.
> Thou who art called the Paraclete
> Best gift of God above,
> The living spring, the living fire,
> Sweet unction and true love.

The promise of the Father

Jesus referred to the Spirit as the promise of the Father (Luke 24:49). In sending the Spirit, God's great promise of our salvation – which is expressed in many different ways in the Bible[1] – reaches fulfilment. But before he fulfilled his promise *through* Christ, he fulfilled it *in* Christ, who became the source of the Spirit for us. In the life of Jesus we see a threefold outpouring of the Holy Spirit:

The Spirit comes at the conception of Jesus

As we shall see later in this chapter, Jesus' first claim about himself was that God had fulfilled his promise and poured out his Spirit (Luke 4:18. 21). Indeed, the Holy Spirit had been active at his very conception. For as the angel announced to Mary: "The Holy Spirit will come upon you... and the power of the Most High will cover you with its shadow" (Luke 1:35). Jesus' very humanity is the result of the Holy Spirit's creative action in our Blessed Lady. This mystery of the Incarnation is at the very centre of our Christian faith, as we

---

1   Isaiah 43:19; Ezekiel 36:26; Jeremiah 31:31; Joel 3:1; John 4:10; 7:37; 14:18; Acts 1:5.

express in the Apostles' Creed: "He was conceived by the power of the Holy Spirit and born of the Virgin Mary". We not only believe that Jesus was the greatest prophet and spiritual leader of all time; we also believe that while being fully human, sharing in all our human weakness, he was the Son of the living God. Although Jesus became like us in all things but sin, there can never be another human being like him in his unique oneness with God. As Pope John Paul II said: "For the Church's faith it is essential and indispensable to affirm that the Word truly "became flesh" and took on *every aspect of humanity*, except sin."[2]

We are not expected to understand how Jesus, whom we see as a baby in his mother's arms, could at the same time be God. Even more challenging, we cannot see how Jesus, dying on the cross, could at the same time be the living God. If we could see his divinity there would be no need for faith. Indeed, as Jesus himself tells us: "No one has ever seen God". We cannot see God with our human eyes. We cannot, therefore, see God in Jesus with our human eyes. His divinity, hidden in his humanity, is disclosed only to the eye of faith.

Faith in Christ's divinity is at the heart of the Christian faith. We have seen how everything that is – ourselves included – was created in and through and for Christ. Sin usurped the very purpose of our creation, in denying that we belonged to Christ. That is why Jesus came, through the power of the Holy Spirit, to save us. And he saves us through the power of that same Spirit through which he became one of us.

The Spirit comes at Jesus' baptism and anointing as Messiah
Jesus was not baptised with the Spirit through the baptism of John the Baptist. Rather, Jesus was at prayer when the Father baptised him in the Holy Spirit (Luke 3:21-22). John himself is the witness: "I saw the Spirit coming down on him from heaven like a dove and resting on him. I did not know him myself, but he who sent me to

---

2   Pope John Paul II, *At the Beginning of the New Millennium* (London: Catholic Truth Society, 2001), 24.

baptise with water had said to me, 'the man on whom you see the Spirit come down and rest is the one who is going to baptise with the Holy Spirit'" (John 1:32-33). The outpouring of the Spirit was the Father's response to Jesus' prayer.

It is surely fitting that on the occasion of the fulfilment of God's promise to pour out his spirit we should get a glimpse of the mystery, not only of the person of Jesus, but also of the God of the promise. When the voice acknowledges Jesus with the words: "You are my Son, the Beloved", it not only confirms John the Baptist's testimony, but also reveals another more profound dimension of the truth about Jesus of Nazareth. It is this: the Messiah is the beloved Son of the Father. This solemn exaltation cannot be reduced to the messianic mission of the Servant of the Lord.[3] There has been a lot of discussion about Jesus' knowledge of himself. Pope John Paul writes:

> However valid it may be to maintain that, because of the human condition which made him grow "in wisdom and in stature, and in favour with God and man", his human awareness of his own mystery would also have progressed to its fullest expression in his glorified humanity, there is no doubt that already in his historical existence Jesus was aware of his identity as the Son of God. John emphasises this to the point of affirming that it was ultimately because of this awareness that Jesus was rejected and condemned: they sought to kill him because he not only broke the Sabbath but also called God his Father, making himself equal with God.[4]

The Spirit empowers Jesus for his mission
Luke tells us that after his baptism Jesus, filled with the Holy Spirit, left the Jordan and was led by the Spirit through the wilderness where he was tempted by the devil (Luke 4:1-13). After overcoming

---

3 *Encyclical on the Holy Spirit*, 19.

4 Pope John Paul II, *At the Beginning of the New Millennium*, 24.

these temptations he returned to Galilee, where he stood up to read in his home synagogue in Nazareth:

> The spirit of the Lord has been given to me,
> for he has anointed me.
> He has sent me to bring the good news to the poor,
> to proclaim liberty to captives
> and to the blind new sight,
> to set the downtrodden free,
> to proclaim the Lord's year of favour (Luke 4:18-19).

Luke catches the atmosphere well: "All eyes in the synagogue were fixed on him" (verse 20). What is he going to say? They all know him as the carpenter's son, but his comment on what he's just read amazes them: "This text is being fulfilled today even as you listen" (verse 21). Jesus is claiming to fulfil God's promise. The Holy Spirit has been poured out on him for his special mission of proclaiming the good news of salvation. It is in the power of the Spirit that Jesus preaches and teaches, heals the sick and casts out evil spirits. Everything he does is empowered by the Spirit. And that same power is with his disciples.

When the disciples return from their first mission and recount to Jesus all that they have accomplished in his name ("even the devils submit to us when we use your name" – Luke 10:17), Jesus has a wonderful experience of the Spirit:

> It was then that, filled with joy by the Holy Spirit, he said: "I bless you, Father, Lord of heaven and earth, for hiding these things from the learned and the clever and revealing them to mere children… Everything has been entrusted to me by my Father; and no one knows who the Son is except the Father, and who the Father is except the Son and those to whom the Son chooses to reveal him" (Luke 10:21-22).

Pope John Paul writes:

> The union of Christ with the Holy Spirit, a union of which
> he is perfectly aware, is expressed in that "rejoicing", which
> in a certain way renders "perceptible" its hidden source.
> Thus there is a particular manifestation and rejoicing
> which is proper to the Son of Man, the Christ-Messiah,
> whose humanity belongs to the person of the Son of God,
> substantially one with the Holy Spirit in divinity.[5]

In his whole being Christ was filled with the Holy Spirit; in all his
ministry he was empowered by the Spirit; in his labours for the
kingdom of God he rejoiced in the Spirit. And he promised that his
disciples would receive the same Spirit and do the same things as
he did: "You will receive power when the Holy Spirit comes on you,
and then you will be my witnesses" (Acts 1:8).

*The Spirit comes on the dead Jesus in the tomb and raises him into
the life of the resurrection*
The Spirit of God, who was so active in Christ throughout his
public ministry, was not absent from his great work through which
he redeemed us, namely, his death on the cross. Scripture tells us
that Christ: "offered himself as the perfect sacrifice to God through
the eternal Spirit" (Hebrews 9:14).

Christ's death was life giving for us because he died through the
power of the Holy Spirit. Through that same Holy Spirit, who is
the Lord, the giver of life, Christ was raised into the new life of
the resurrection. Filled with the new life of the resurrection, by the
power of the Holy Spirit, Jesus came to his disciples in the upper
room on Easter Sunday evening and greeted them with the words
"Peace be with you." Then he said: "As the Father sent me, so am
I sending you" (John 20:21). Next he breathed on them and said:
"Receive the Holy Spirit. For those whose sins you forgive, they are

---

5 *Encyclical on the Holy Spirit*, 21.

forgiven; for those whose sins you retain, they are retained" (verses 22-23).

Jesus gives to his disciples the same gift which he had received from the Father. He empowers them with the same power with which he had been empowered by the Father. He entrusts to them the same mission which he had received from the Father – the mission of preaching the Gospel. What Jesus did through the power of the Spirit, he continued through his disciples because he had given them his Spirit.

In the resurrection Jesus receives the fullness of the Spirit for us. As Peter said: "Now raised to the heights by God's right hand, he has received from the Father the Holy Spirit, who was promised, and what you see and hear is the outpouring of that Spirit" (Acts 2:33). The promise is fulfilled, first of all in the person of Our Lord Jesus Christ. In that fulfilment Christ becomes the New Adam, the source of renewed and restored humanity. As Paul said: "The last Adam has become a life-giving spirit" (1 Corinthians 15:45). Tom Smail comments:

> The last Adam, the ultimate man, is the one who has been transfigured and sanctified by the Spirit so as to fulfil at last God's purpose for the whole of humanity. As such he is so full of the Spirit of divine self-giving that he pours out upon others his transfigured and fulfilled humanity, so that they also may be changed into sanctified and fulfilled people.[6]

The Holy Spirit "makes" the Church

The mystery of Pentecost is the mystery of the Church. The Second Vatican Council made it clear that the Church is established when the Spirit is poured out:

> By communicating his Spirit to his brothers, called together from all people, Christ made them mystically his own body.[7]

---

6 Smail, *The Giving Gift*, 105.

7 Second Vatican Council, *Lumen Gentium* [Constitution on the Church], 7.

Rising from the dead, he sent his life-giving Spirit upon his disciples and through this Spirit has established his body, the Church, as the universal sacrament of salvation.[8]

After being lifted up on the cross and glorified, the Lord Jesus poured forth the Spirit whom he had promised and through whom he called and gathered the people of the New Covenant.[9]

The Council teaches that the Church is the direct result of Christ's action of sending the Spirit. Pentecost is the birth of the Church. Just as Jesus himself was born through the power of the Holy Spirit, so the Church of Christ is born through that same Holy Spirit. The Church is God's plan for our salvation. We cannot separate Christ from the Church, nor can we separate the Holy Spirit from the Church, because Christ and the Spirit are co-creative of, and co-responsible for, the Church. It was not God's will to save us simply as individuals. The Vatican Council teaches:

God has willed to make people holy and save them, not as individuals without any bond or link between them, but rather to make them into a people who might acknowledge him and serve him in holiness.[10]

Clearly, it is as members of the Church that we are saved and sanctified. The first action of the Spirit is to make us one – the Body of Christ. As Pope Benedict XVI wrote while he was still a professor of theology: "Teaching about the Church must take its departure from teaching about the Holy Spirit and his gifts".[11]

Sometimes you meet people who call themselves Christians but who have rejected the Church. They believe that they can have Christ without his Church. They may be fed up with the human

---

8 *Lumen Gentium*, 40.

9 *Decree on Ecumenism*, 2.

10 *Lumen Gentium*, 9.

11 Joseph Ratzinger, *Introduction to Christianity* (2nd ed.) (San Francisco: Ignatius Press, 2004), 333.

weaknesses which abound in the Church. They are not prepared to reflect on the obvious fact that the Church is made up of ordinary human beings, with all their weaknesses, and it is upon these ordinary, weak human men and women that Jesus pours out his Spirit. If the Church is not flawless and perfect they will have nothing more to do with it! They are really saying that they want Christ without the mystery of Pentecost, without the outpouring of the Holy Spirit. They want to listen to Christ, without listening to the Church, even though Christ said to his disciples:

> Go, therefore, make disciples of all the nations, baptise them in the name of the Father and of the Son and of the Holy Spirit, and teach them to observe all the commands I gave you. And know that I am with you always; yes, to the end of time (Matthew 28:19-20).

It is very sad when members of the Church, who have been anointed with the Holy Spirit and who have been called to live a life of love and service, fail in their calling and live selfish, unrepentant lives. But it is no justification for rejecting the Church of Christ. Anyone who reflects on the mystery of the outpouring of the Holy Spirit on ordinary, weak and sinful men and women, who have the personal freedom to make their own decisions, will be pained when members of the Church, especially leaders, use their freedom to act sinfully, but they will not reject the Church. Because to do so would be to suggest that Christ ought to have deprived sinful people of their free will before he gave them the Holy Spirit.

God's Spirit in our hearts
The Spirit is the proof that we have become the children of God. Paul said:

> The proof that you are sons is that God has sent the Spirit of his Son into our hearts: the Spirit that cries, "Abba, Father",

and it is this that makes you a son, you are not a slave any more (Galatians 4:6-7).

The Spirit is Christ's first gift to us. The Spirit within us enables us to acknowledge what Christ has achieved for us: we acknowledge that we have become children of God through Christ when we call God "Abba". And when we do this, then "it is that very Spirit bearing witness with our spirit that we are children of God" (Romans 8:16).

We need the Spirit in order to pray "Abba". But we also need the Spirit to acknowledge that Jesus is Lord. Our human reason alone cannot give us the assurance that we are children of God – it can only come through the Spirit. The Spirit brings to our consciousness the awareness that we are God's children and prays within us. As Tom Smail writes we must pray this prayer *for ourselves* but we cannot pray it *by ourselves*.[12] None of us can decide, simply by our own reason, to accept God as our loving Father. That acceptance, that recognition, comes from the presence of the Holy Spirit in our hearts. In the same way, the Spirit also brings to our consciousness the fact that Jesus is now seated at the right hand of the Father and enables us to acknowledge this mystery by proclaiming, "Jesus Christ is Lord". The confession of the lordship of Jesus comes through the grace of the Spirit's personal presence in our hearts. We must make this profession that Jesus is Lord for ourselves, but we cannot make it by ourselves. This profession is the work of grace. Without the grace of faith all the study in the world will not enable us to proclaim that Jesus is Lord. As Tom Smail points out:

> The techniques of biblical scholarship can certainly bring us to a more accurate appreciation of what the biblical writers are saying; but, to bring us to the conviction of the truth of the Gospel and a relationship with the God of whom it speaks, is the prerogative of the Holy Spirit alone.[13]

---

12 Smail, *The Giving Gift*, 173.

13 As above.

Two short phrases, then, highlight the major work of the Holy Spirit in our hearts. Through the Holy Spirit we can call God our loving Father, our "Abba", and through the same Spirit we can proclaim that Jesus is now Lord of all. We should hold on with great confidence to what Paul tells us about this praying activity of the Spirit in our hearts:

> The Spirit too comes to help us in our weakness. For when we cannot choose words in order to pray properly, the Spirit himself expresses our plea in a way that could never be put into words, and God who knows everything in our hearts knows perfectly well what he means, and that the pleas of the saints expressed by the Spirit are according to the mind of God (Romans 8:26-27).

Our hearts are full of prayer, not our own prayer, and not our own very inadequate words of prayer, but the eternal prayer of the Holy Spirit, interceding for us and bringing our deepest needs to our loving Father. The Spirit cries, "Abba". That is the prayer of Jesus. The Spirit is not the son of the Father: Jesus is. The Spirit produces in us the prayer which he produces in the heart of Jesus. Now, in the same Spirit we can pray with Jesus, "Abba, Father". As André Louf said:

> We received prayer along with grace in our baptism. The state of grace, as we call it, at the level of the heart actually signifies a state of prayer. From then on in the profoundest depths of the self, we have a continuing contact with God. God's Holy Spirit has taken us over, has assumed complete possession of us; he has become breath of our breath and Spirit of our spirit. He takes our heart in tow and turns it towards God... This state of prayer within us is something we always carry about with us, like a hidden treasure of which we are not consciously aware. Somewhere our heart is going full pelt, but we do not feel it. We are deaf to our praying heart.[14]

---

14 Smail, *The Giving Gift*, 209.

Pause for a moment now. Ask the Holy Spirit to come. Listen to his voice as he prays "Abba, Father". And, as you join your voice with his in calling God your loving Father, proclaim also that Jesus is Lord. Then become aware of the great mystery that the Holy Spirit is praying in your very weakness. And reflect on the amazing truth that despite your own sinfulness God's Holy Spirit dwells in your heart.

The sanctifying role of the Spirit

The primary role of the Holy Spirit is the sanctification of God's people. As Tom Smail puts it:

> The distinctive work of the Spirit is to communicate to us the life that is in the Father and the Son, so that we actually share and experience it in ourselves. In the Spirit the life that the Father wills and that the Son incarnates is brought over to our side of our relationship with them and begins to reach its destination in us as the first fruits of the whole human race for which it was intended.[15]

When the Spirit of God comes to dwell in us at our baptism, we are filled with the whole life of God. We are, in the words of Jesus, "born of water and the Spirit" (John 3:5). We become the people of the new covenant.

St Thomas Aquinas, seven hundred years ago, was clearly identifying the new covenant with the Holy Spirit when he wrote: "The New Covenant consists in the in-pouring of the Holy Spirit."[16] He also wrote:

> That which is preponderant in the law of the New Covenant and whereon all its efficacy is based, is the grace of the Holy Spirit, which is given through faith in Christ. Consequently the New Law is chiefly the grace itself of the Holy Spirit.[17]

---

15 Smail, *The Giving Gift*, 167.

16 St Thomas Aquinas, *Commentary on Hebrews*, Cap 8, lect. 2.

17 St Thomas Aquinas, *Summa Theologica*, 1 -11, 106 art 1.

Because the new law is chiefly the grace of the Holy Spirit, it, unlike the old law, justifies us. It makes us holy because the law itself is the very presence of the sanctifying Holy Spirit.

We are the people of the new covenant, in other words the people of the Holy Spirit, whose interior law of action is the Spirit of God. The new law is the sanctifying, dynamic presence of the Holy Spirit. That is why Paul can say: "If we live by the Spirit let us also be guided by the Spirit" (Galatians 5:25). Our Christian morality is not a slavish following of laws; it is a joyful, free response to the Spirit of God who wants to transform us into the perfect image of Christ. Jesus identified three things which the Spirit would do:

> And when he comes,
> he will show the world how wrong it was,
> about sin,
> and about who was in the right,
> and about judgement:
> about sin:
> proved by their refusal to believe in me;
> about who was in the right:
> proved by my going to the Father
> and your seeing me no more;
> about judgement:
> proved by the prince of this world being already condemned
> (John 16:8-11).

The Spirit convicts us of sin

Scripture says: "The heart is more devious than any other thing" (Jeremiah 17:9). The sinful heart cannot admit its sinfulness. It is only the light of the Spirit which can dispel the darkness of sin. The Spirit, sent among us for the forgiveness of sin, prepares our heart for this gift by enabling us to acknowledge our sinfulness and say with the publican in the temple: "God, be merciful to me, a sinner" (Luke 18:13). Pope John Paul wrote:

Conversion requires convincing of sin; it includes the interior judgement of the conscience, and this, being a proof of the action of the Spirit of truth in man's inmost being, becomes at the same time a new beginning of the bestowal of grace and love: "Receive the Holy Spirit". Thus in the "convincing concerning sin" we discover a double gift: the gift of the truth of conscience and the gift of the certainty of redemption. The Spirit of truth is the Counsellor.[18]

The Holy Spirit, then, is the new covenant; the guarantee that we are the children of God; by enabling us to call God "Abba" and proclaim that Jesus is Lord, he simultaneously fills us with the life of God and convicts us of our sinfulness so that we can turn to God and have our sins forgiven. The Holy Spirit is our divine friend and protector, guide and sanctifier, encourager and comforter. And he wants to have a loving, personal relationship with each of us.

My brother Sean, a Redemptorist priest in Washington, came into a new personal relationship with the Holy Spirit one night as he was praying about the troubles in Northern Ireland. For over thirty years he had been working through the American Congress for political action to address the deep causes of conflict. His prayer was for peace. The Lord answered his prayer in a very personal way, by keeping him awake one night, filling his heart with praise and gratitude and giving him this prayer of commitment in his heart:

> All powerful-gentle,
> faithful-gracious,
> crucified-risen,
> L I V I N G
> Lord Jesus,
> Send me your Spirit.
>
> Lord of History,
> Lord of the world,

---

18 *Encyclical on the Holy Spirit*, 31.

Lord of Ireland,
Lord of my heart,
pour out your Spirit upon me.

Lord Jesus,
I am an empty vessel,
parched and thirsty,
waiting to be filled.
Fill me with your living water
that I may never thirst again.

Risen Jesus,
baptise me in your Spirit
so that I can truly call God,
Abba, Father.
Come Holy Spirit, come
take possession of my soul
and make it all thine own.

Come living flame divine,
consume this heart of mine,
come holy breath of God,
breathe on me your life.

Come dwell with me,
Holy Paraclete,
my Counsellor and my Guide,
come, heal my heart and mind.

This prayer bubbled up within him, and kept him in the presence of God the whole night. It gave him a whole new relationship with God, a personal relationship. Jesus wants each of us to have an intimate, personal relationship with God our Father, a loving acknowledgement that he is Lord and a grateful awareness that the Holy Spirit in our hearts is the Lord, the giver of life.

Personal spiritual exercise

- Centre yourself, using the techniques we learned in week one.
- Bring yourself to bodily stillness and calm.
- Now ask yourself: Do I really wish Jesus to baptise me in the Holy Spirit? Will I ask him for this blessing in the Spirit?
- Now focus again on your breathing.
- And bring yourself gently back to the world.

8

Life in the Spirit

In the last chapter we reflected on the sanctifying role of the Holy Spirit. The Spirit is the Lord the giver of life, our eternal life. God is love and the first gift the Spirit gives us is love: "The love of God has been poured into our hearts by the Holy Spirit which has been given us" (Romans 5:5). The Spirit comes to us so that we can be reborn as children of God. In our hearts the Spirit cries out "Abba, Father"; the Spirit enables us to proclaim that Jesus is Lord. The Spirit is, as St Thomas Aquinas said, the new covenant. In the words of the liturgy: "The Holy Spirit is sent among us for the forgiveness of our sins". At one and the same time the Spirit convicts us of sin and, as we say in one of the post-communion prayers at Mass, "The Holy Spirit is the forgiveness of sins." All this work of the Holy Spirit is for our sanctification.

We are called to be holy. As St Paul said, God chose us in Christ to be "holy and spotless, and to live through love in his presence" (Ephesians 1:4). In baptism we are united to Christ. We receive the life of Christ, the very life of God. We become members of Christ's body. St John Eudes had a very clear understanding of what this involves. He wrote:

Remember that our Lord Jesus Christ is your true head and that you are his members. He is to you as the head is to the members of the body; all that is his is yours. His spirit, his heart, his body, his soul, all his faculties, all are to be used by you as if they were your own, so that serving him you may praise him, love him, glorify him. For your part, you are to him as a member to the head, and he earnestly desires to use all your faculties as if they were his own for the service and glorification of his Father.[1]

Personal holiness is the fruit of our sharing fully in Christ's mission, doing Christ's work on earth in the way in which he himself did it, namely through the power of the Holy Spirit. The Vatican Council, for instance, said: "Priests will acquire holiness in their own distinctive way by exercising their functions sincerely and tirelessly in the Spirit of Christ."[2] Each member of the Church acquires holiness by the way in which he or she lives out their vocation – married, single or religious, in union with the Spirit of Jesus.

The Spirit fills us with sanctifying grace. But the Spirit also empowers us to make Christ known to others. We call this charismatic grace, the grace which enables us to do the work of Christ. In the fourth Eucharistic prayer the Church prays:

That we might live no longer for ourselves but for him,
he sent the Holy Spirit from you, Father,
as his first gift to those who believe,
to complete his work on earth
and bring us the fullness of grace.

The Spirit comes to complete Christ's work in and through each member of his body, the Church. And just as the Spirit empowered Jesus for his work when he was anointed at the Jordan, so the Spirit

---

1   Office of Readings, 19 August, Feast of St John Eudes.

2   Second Vatican Council, *Presbyterorum Ordinis* [Decree on the ministry and life of Priests], 13.

empowers us when we are anointed, especially in the sacraments of baptism and confirmation. Jesus promised that empowerment: "John baptised with water but you, not many days from now, will be baptised with the Holy Spirit… you will receive power when the Holy Spirit comes on you, and then you will be my witnesses" (Acts 1:5. 8).

A young man in Jos, in Northern Nigeria, gave me a vivid illustration of this. He was selling crocodile skin bags and purses. I approached his stall with a friend, who is a priest and theologian, and we began to bargain. To our surprise he wouldn't lower his price and we were about to move on. "One moment," he said, "I am not here to sell bags." At that he reached beneath his stall and took out two leaflets. He handed them to us and asked my friend, "Have you received the new heart?" Somewhat taken aback, my friend replied, "I think I have." The young man responded immediately, "What do you mean, you think you have? If you have, you know; if you don't know, you haven't!" My friend, now quite flustered, asked, "Well, have you received the new heart?" The young man said, with great confidence, "Yes, I have." "How do you know?" asked my friend. And with calm assurance the young man replied, "Because I have the power to witness to Jesus."

Jesus had promised: "You will receive power," and the Spirit had come. The proof was in the fact that he was an evangelist. He was trying to make Christ known.

Charisms

This empowerment of the Holy Spirit manifests itself in what Paul called charisms. Paul coined this Greek word, which means "work of grace", to describe the activity of the Holy Spirit in the lives of Christians. He wrote to the Corinthians:

> There is a variety of gifts but always the same Spirit; there are all sorts of service to be done, but always to the same Lord; working in all sorts of different ways in different

people, it is the same God who is working in all of them. The particular way in which the Spirit is given to each person is for a good purpose. One may have the gift of preaching with wisdom, given him by the Spirit; another may have the gift of preaching instruction given him by the same Spirit; and another the gift of faith given by the same Spirit; another again the gift of healing, through this one Spirit; one, the power of miracles; another, prophecy; another the gift of recognising spirits; another the gift of tongues and another the ability to interpret them. All these are the work of one and the same Spirit, who distributes different gifts to different people just as he chooses (1 Corinthians 12:4-11).

We call these "charismatic gifts" or "graces". The Holy Spirit gives us two distinct graces:

Sanctifying grace
This makes us the children of God. This is the gift of eternal life, and our salvation depends on it. As Paul said: "The Spirit himself and our spirit bear united witness that we are children of God. And if we are children we are heirs as well: heirs of God and coheirs with Christ, sharing his sufferings, so as to share his glory" (Romans 8:16-17). That is what we call sanctifying grace a whole new friendship and love with God.

Charismatic grace
This enables us to serve others and empowers us to fulfil the mission that Christ has entrusted to each of us. Like the young man in Jos, it enables us to say: "I have the power to witness to Jesus." Without it, none of us would have the strength to witness to Christ. The word "martyr", which we use to describe people who have died for their faith, comes from the Greek word meaning "witness". A martyr is a witness. And without the power that the Holy Spirit gives no one would have the strength to give that witness to Christ. For witness we need the charismatic gifts of the Holy Spirit.

We need both graces, because through sanctifying grace we *live* in union with God, while through charismatic grace we *work* in union with God. To put it another way: through sanctifying grace the Holy Spirit works to keep us united to God and make us members of Christ; while through charismatic grace the Holy Spirit works in us, as members of Christ, to keep us serving the kingdom of God. Pope John Paul II pointed to the charisms of the Spirit as one of the signs of hope in our world today:

> In the Church the signs of hope include a greater attention to the voice of the Spirit through the acceptance of charisms and the promotion of the laity, a deeper commitment to the cause of Christian unity and the increased interest in dialogue with other religions and with contemporary culture.[3]

For centuries there was a strong conviction in the Church that the charisms should not be expected in our day. Even in the Vatican Council this opinion was voiced by Cardinal Ruffini. According to the theologian Killian McDonald, Ruffini believed that such gifts today are "extremely rare and altogether exceptional", and that charisms "have no important role to play in the life of the modern Church."[4]

But Ruffini's view did not prevail. In fact, the Council rejected it in most emphatic terms. In its major document on the Church it teaches:

> It is not only through the sacraments and Church ministries that the same Holy Spirit sanctifies and leads the People of God and enriches it with virtues. Allotting his gifts "to everyone according to his will" (1 Corinthians 12:11), he distributes special graces among the faithful of every rank. By these gifts he makes them fit and ready to undertake various tasks and offices advantageous for the renewal and upbuilding of the Church... These charismatic gifts, whether they be the most

---

3 Apostolic Letter, *Tertio Millennium Adveniente*, 46.

4 K. McDonald, *The Holy Spirit and Power* (New York: Doubleday & Co Inc., 1975), 123.

outstanding or the more simple and widely diffused, are to be received with thanksgiving and consolation, for they are exceedingly suitable and useful for the needs of the Church.[5]

Francis Sullivan SJ proposes this definition:

A charism can be described as a grace-given capacity and willingness for some kind of service that contributes to the renewal of and upbuilding of the Church.[6]

In contrast with Ruffini's desire, forty years ago, to see all mention of charisms eliminated, the Church today has a broad experience of the charisms at work in men and women in every walk of life. Indeed, in his very first encyclical Pope John Paul wrote:

The powers of the Spirit, the gifts of the Spirit, and the fruits of the Holy Spirit are revealed in men. The present-day Church seems to repeat with ever greater fervour and with holy insistence: Come, Holy Spirit! Come! Come! Heal our wounds, our strength renew; On our dryness pour your dew; Wash the stains of guilt away; Mend the stubborn heart and will; Melt the frozen, warm the chill; Guide the hearts that go astray.[7]

This "holy insistence" in calling on the Spirit to come has become a transforming prayer in the lives of millions of men and women throughout the Church. They have found their lives changed; they witness to a deeper experience of God; they begin to use new gifts of the Spirit and become involved in ministries at every level in their communities. Their transforming experience is frequently called "baptism in the Spirit".

---

5   *Lumen Gentium*, 12.

6   Francis Sullivan, *Charisms and Charismatic Renewal: a Biblical and Theological study* (Ann Arbor, MI: Servant Books, 1982), 13.

7   *Redemptor Hominis*, 8.

Baptism in the Spirit

It is through baptism that we become members of the Church of Christ, members of the Body of Christ, and our bodies become temples of the Holy Spirit. Baptism is the great sacrament of salvation, the sacrament that opens the door of all the other sacraments and is the foundation of all Christian life. When we hear the phrase "baptism in the Spirit", we are not hearing about anything new, or different, or more powerful than the sacrament we know. We are rediscovering one of the ways in which the Holy Spirit in our time is renewing the Church and its individual members by bringing to life the grace and gifts that are received in baptism and confirmation.

Faith and grace are not "things" that the Church gives us in baptism and which we can, as it were, keep in the bank. They are dimensions of our relationship with God – a living, personal relationship. Faith gives us knowledge of God and enables us to know God in the depths of our being. It enables us to trust and approach God with confidence and call him Father. Grace, what we normally call sanctifying grace, is the very life of God within us, the life that Jesus refers to when he says: "I have come so that they may have life and have it to the full" (John 10:10). This abundant life infuses our whole being with the peace of God. Grace assures us that we are loved and accepted. Being in the state of grace is living in the love of God, confidently calling him Father, and opening our whole life to the redeeming and empowering presence of the Spirit. Losing the state of grace, through wilful sin, is the greatest disaster that can befall a human being. God took the risk of creating us with freedom and inviting us to live in love and friendship with him. The most soul-destroying response is to reject that love and live locked in the prison of our own selfishness. That is "living in sin". When someone cuts him- or herself off from the abundant life of God and lives a disintegrated and disorientated life, with self-gratification or self-aggrandisement as their only goal, that is really "hell on earth".

We receive both faith and grace in the sacrament of baptism. But it has been the experience of many people that these gifts, instead of being on fire with enthusiasm, remain cold and even dormant. They know in their hearts that they want to be faithful to God, want to love and serve God. But somehow zeal and enthusiasm evade them. They say their prayers, but often without conviction; they go to Mass, but often just out of duty. The God in whom they believe, and whom they want to serve, seems far away. And very often Christ seems to be someone in the past. Intuitively they know that their faith is the great gift of God and they often experience deep yearning in their heart for a more personal relationship with God. But how can they get that relationship? What can set their faith on fire?

Many people have begun to act in new ways on Jesus' promise to be with them when two or three meet (Matthew 18:20). They meet in small prayer groups, acknowledge the presence of Jesus and confess that Jesus alone baptises in the Holy Spirit. They pray over each other, asking the Father, in Jesus' name, to fill them afresh with the Spirit. And he does. The Father honours Jesus' promise and pours out the Spirit afresh. They pray not only for a fresh outpouring of the Spirit but for the release of all the gifts of the Spirit which were already given in baptism and in confirmation. These gifts of the Spirit are essential for doing the work of Christ.

When someone is baptised as an infant and confirmed at a young age, it undoubtedly brings them the new life of Christ and the gift of the Spirit. But at the same time she or he may not have ratified that commitment, which was made on their behalf by their sponsors, as a free and mature adult. Some people live as practising Catholics for many years, without ever saying: "Jesus, I accept you as my Lord and Saviour and I ask you to unite me more deeply to yourself by filling me with your Spirit. Jesus, release within me all the many gifts of the Spirit you gave me when I was baptised and confirmed."

When someone is led to say this prayer and make this commitment in the presence of others, the Lord always answers. Sometimes the answer can be quite dramatic. Some people witness to great experiences of peace and joy and inner healing;

of experiencing God's love in a new way, and beginning to live in new ways as Christians. Others say that they've had no tangible experience at all, and yet they know, deep down, that something very profound has happened.

I had my own experience of baptism in the Spirit on 24 September 1975, the feast of Our Lady of Mercy. I was directing the first Three-Month Renewal Course at Hawkstone Hall for Priests and Religious. I had invited Fr Francis Sullivan SJ, Dean of the Gregorian University in Rome and a leading theologian, to give a week on the Charisms of the Spirit. I was aware that a new renewal movement, known as Catholic Pentecostalism, was big news in America, and that Fr Sullivan had written a substantial article on baptism in the Spirit – an experience which he said was at the heart of the movement.

Word spread about the course, and on the Sunday evening thirty card-carrying charismatics showed up. The first thing they did on arrival was to hold a prayer meeting. At the time I had no experience of this kind of prayer, but I was deeply impressed by their sincerity and the way they spoke to Jesus. But I was deeply challenged when they started singing and speaking in tongues, and retreated upstairs. I remember a few of us joking about what we had let into the house – aware that we had a whole week to go.

On Monday morning Fr Sullivan began his lectures. He gave us a very fine overview of Pentecostalism and how this spirituality had reached the Catholic Church. It was clear that he was a systematic theologian, who carefully avoided exaggeration. Prayer meetings and prayers for healing were held each day, as well as the exposition of the blessed sacrament. I was amazed at how keen people were for an hour and a half of silent adoration. I was deeply challenged. I wanted to share their joy in the Lord, but I was afraid to give the Lord the freedom to act in me as he willed.

On Wednesday, during the Holy Hour, I could no longer resist. I said to the Lord that I would ask the first priest who walked out of the church to pray with me and hear my confession. The first priest was Fr Wilfred Brieven, from Belgium, who was acting as the delegate of Cardinal Suenens[8]. When I approached him he said, "Let's go now," and we went to my office. I told him about my dialogue with the Lord. I then knelt down and made my confession, just as I had done all my life. Then something quite new happened. Instead of simply giving me absolution, Fr Brieven imposed hands on me and began to sing and pray in tongues. He gave praise to God for anointing me as a priest and asked Jesus to send the Holy Spirit afresh and renew within me all the grace of the priesthood. As he prayed I began to experience God's Spirit healing deep areas of my life and giving me a new assurance that I was precious in God's sight. In fact, in that moment the Spirit gave me the grace that has shaped my whole ministry ever since. It has influenced my preaching, teaching and sacramental ministry, especially in the sacrament of confession, as well as my whole approach to healing ministry.

In that sacramental moment with Fr Brieven I experienced in my own heart everything that Fr Sullivan was teaching. The charisms of the Spirit are alive and active today and are given to us for the work of preaching the Gospel. Fr Sullivan's definition aptly describes what I experienced:

> Baptism in the Spirit is a religious experience which initiates a decisively new sense of the powerful presence and working of God in one's life, which working usually involves one or more charismatic gifts.[9]

Up until that point my pastoral approach, though based on theology, was dominated by ideas about pastoral psychology and sociology. Afterwards my ministry began to be based on God's word and the power of the Holy Spirit. I became convinced that all ministry in the name of Jesus had to be based on the word of God. It means

---

8 Cardinal Suenens had been mandated by Pope Paul VI to watch over the growth and development of the Charismatic Renewal in the Church.

9 Sullivan, *Charisms and Charismatic Renewal: a Biblical and Theological study*, 13.

that no pastoral situation is too daunting, because the power to respond to it doesn't come from my own knowledge or skills, but from Christ. The gifts of the Spirit, the charisms that were needed in each new pastoral situation, would be given as the Spirit saw fit.

A conversion experience

Reflecting on how the Lord gave me that experience of baptism in the Spirit has enabled me to encourage others to be open to Christ in each new situation. Don't set limits on grace! Grace knows no boundaries once we are open to the Spirit. Becoming open to the Spirit is what we mean by being converted. The heart that is converted is open to receive the Spirit of God in a new way. Conversion is my response to God's call in Christ. It is my willingness to accept the kingdom and live by the values of the kingdom. Conversion brings a radical change in the direction of our lives and in the motivation in what we do. Conversion is the way we accept the new life that Jesus came to bring us.

The Greek Fathers spoke about the new life given by the Spirit in terms of divinisation. Through grace we become not just "pleasing to God" – we become divinised ourselves. And that is the very goal of our existence. We were created in God's image and our vocation is to become like God. We cannot do this without a radical conversion, because without being divinised to the depths of our being, Christ cannot do what he wants to do in our hearts.

Conversion is not an abstract concept, but takes place on many levels. Its essence is taking responsibility for every area of our lives; emotionally, intellectually, morally and socially, as well as for our Christian and religious lives. As Donald Gelpi SJ writes: "I define conversion as the decision to reject irresponsible choices and to assume responsibility for one's subsequent development in some area of human experience".[10]

The first step is to take responsibility for the grace of baptism. The second step is acknowledge that only God can satisfy the deep

---

10 Donald Gelpi SJ, *Grace as Transmuted Experience and Social Process* (Lanham, Maryland: University Press of America, 1988), 102.

yearning in our hearts. And the third step is to recognise that the thirst in our lives is really for the Spirit of God. Once we begin to take these steps, no matter how hesitatingly, we are opening our hearts for the grace that is called baptism in the Spirit. We begin to live life in the Spirit.

Personal spiritual exercise

- Centre yourself, using the techniques we learned in week one.
- Bring yourself to bodily stillness and calm.
- Now ask yourself: Am I really open to receive from God the gifts of the Sprit that I need for my life and witness as Christ's disciple? Am I ready to receive the gift God wants to give me now?
- Ask God to fill you with the gifts of the Spirit.
- Now be still.
- Now focus again on your breathing.
- And bring yourself gently back to the world.

9

The Indwelling of God in Our Hearts

When I reflect on all the great promises which God has made through Christ, I always feel that this one is the greatest:

> If anyone loves me he will keep my word,
> and my Father will love him,
> and we shall come to him
> and make our home with him (John 14:23).

When I hear that promise, I ask the same question that Mary did when she heard that she had been chosen to be the mother of God: "How can this come about?" (Luke 1:34). The answer is the same that Mary received: "The Holy Spirit will come upon you." It is in the Holy Spirit that the Father and the Son take up their residence in our hearts.

The Vatican Council said: "In reality it is only in the mystery of the Word made flesh that the mystery of humanity truly becomes clear."[1] The mystery of humanity, the mystery of each man and woman, is this profound presence of God in the human heart.

---

1 Second Vatican Council, *Gaudium et Spes* [Constitution on the Church in the Modern World], 22.

That is truly amazing news, Pope John Paul II said: "In reality, the name for that deep amazement at man's worth and dignity is the Gospel, that is to say: the Good News. It is also called Christianity."[2] We know about this presence because Jesus Christ has revealed it to us. But this is not just a revelation about God; it is a revelation about ourselves. Without revelation we would never have known this amazing truth which transforms both our image of God and the way we value and esteem ourselves. Each and every person you meet is the temple of God, and your own body is the temple of the Holy Spirit. These revealed truths have the power to shape and change the way we see and experience ourselves and others. As the Orthodox Patriarch Bartholomew 1 of Constantinople said to the Synod of Bishops in Rome:

> The example of saints is the tangible experience and human expression of God's love in our community. In the gentle presence of a saint we learn how theology and action coincide. In the compassionate love of the saint, we experience God as "our father" and God's mercy as steadfastly enduring. Each of us is called to "become like fire", to touch the world with the mystical force of God's word so that – as the extended Body of Christ – the world, too, might say: "Someone touched me".[3]

Becoming alive to the indwelling presence of God in every human heart, even in our greatest enemy, compels us to show respect and radically change how we see and evaluate other people. It also transforms the way we evaluate our own lives. But sadly, we can keep these truths from entering our conscious awareness. St Augustine lamented: "Too late have I loved you, O Beauty so ancient and so new, too late have I loved you! Behold, you were within me, while I was outside."[4] Augustine's liberating discovery was that the God he sought was not at a distance. God was within.

---

2 *Redemptor Hominis*, 10.

3 Address to Synod, 7 October 2008.

4 St Augustine, *Confessions*, 10, 27.

If we do not dwell happily with God, who is within, I begin to live outside myself. So I am escaping not only from the God within, but also from myself.

The search for God, as St Augustine discovered, takes a very personal and inward turn. We don't find God by imagining some heaven far beyond our human experience. Rather, we find God by entering our own hearts and discovering God at the very core of our human experience and history. Right there, in the midst of your deepest yearning and striving, at the heart of our passion for justice, peace and fraternity, at the very core of our best ambitions for ourselves and those we love, God is present. God is not absent from anything that is good, from all the human emotions that he created. The struggle of the spiritual journey is not to get beyond ourselves, in some form of ecstasy, but to come within ourselves and take possession of ourselves. As we embark on this inner journey we encounter many obstacles, all of our own making. They can all be seen as manifestations of what mystical writers like Thomas Merton called the "false self", which is really a false understanding of our true worth and dignity. We are tempted to use false criteria for evaluating ourselves. We tend to judge ourselves in the light of three things: what we have, what we do and what others think of us. Those things are not within us; they are extrinsic to the human heart. God indwells the heart, the true self.

The spiritual journey begins for each of us in earnest as we turn to make that inward move, not to the neglect of everything that is going on around us, but in order to get the correct perspective on what is happening in our lives. As Pope Benedict XVI said:

> Man knows himself only when he learns to understand himself in the light of God, and he knows others only when he sees the mystery of God in them.[5]

When we are caught up in the heat of the moment, we very easily lose sight of the divine reality at the heart of each person. The

---

5 Pope Benedict, *Jesus of Nazareth*, 282.

mystery in the depths of everyone is the divine indwelling of the Holy Trinity. If we lose sight of this mystery we begin to evaluate and judge everything in relation to ourselves alone. And we end up reducing the world to very small proportions indeed, because the "false self" is on a collision course with the common good. Everyone on the spiritual journey has to make the same discovery: our true good is the common good. As the Vatican Council said: "We can discover our true self only in sincere self-giving."[6] Our very capacity to make the sincere gift of self, of seeking communion with the other, is the clearest sign that we are made in the image of the triune God, Father, Son and Holy Spirit.

God, who is a divine communion of Persons, creates us in his own image and thereby makes us capable of becoming a communion of persons. No one can be born in isolation. In fact, we can say that being in communion with others is intrinsic to what it means to be a person. This is what it means to be made in the image of God. When God, who is a communion of divine Persons, creates us in his own image and likeness he inscribes within us both the capacity for and the need for being in a communion of persons.

The Church owes a great debt to Pope John Paul II, who, between 1979 and 1984, devoted five years of Catechesis to exploring the image of God in men and women. During those years he gave 129 General Audience addresses on what he called "the theology of the body". He set himself the task of providing an "adequate anthropology", a faith-inspired way of seeing and understanding the human person. These addresses have now been published as *Man and Woman He Created Them: A Theology of the Body*.[7] This major contribution to the theological understanding of what it means to be human has opened up a whole new field of study.

Traditionally we have been taught that the soul is made in the image of God, but with no mention of the body. Indeed, St Thomas Aquinas taught very specifically that "to be the image of God

---

6 *Gaudium et Spes*, 22.

7 Pope John Paul II, *Man and Woman He Created Them: A Theology of the Body*, Trans. Michael Waldstein (Boston: Pauline Books & Media, 2006).

belongs to the mind only".[8] By contrast, Pope John Paul was very clear that the human body, the whole person is made in the image of God. He wrote:

> In the mystery of creation, the human body carried within itself an unquestionable sign of the "image of God" and also constituted the specific source of the certainty of this image, present in the whole human being. In a way, original acceptance of the body was the basis of the acceptance of the whole visible world.[9]

The body is not simply a biology; it is a theology and a sacramental reality. Pope John Paul says:

> In man, created in the image of God, the very sacramentality of creation, the sacramentality of the world, was in some way revealed. In fact, through his bodiliness, his masculinity and femininity, man becomes a visible sign of the economy of truth and love, which has its source in God himself and was revealed already in the mystery of creation.[10]

The human body manifests and reveals the human person. You don't have a body; in a real sense you are your body. What is done to your body is done to you. Indeed, the human body reveals both the human person and God. Again Pope John Paul says:

> The human body, in fact, and only the body, is capable of making visible what is invisible: the spiritual and divine. It was created to transfer into the visible reality of the world, the mystery hidden from eternity in God, and thus to be a sign of it.[11]

---

8 St Thomas Aquinas, *Summa Theologica* 1:Q 93, art. 6.

9 Pope John Paul II, *Man and Woman He Created Them: A Theology of the Body*, 27:3.

10 As above, 19:5.

11 As above, 19:4.

That is the fundamental thesis of Pope John Paul's whole theology of the body. The body reveals the invisible reality of the spiritual, of the divine. But the body, manifesting the person, can only exist in relationship, in a communion of persons. So, the image of God in the human person is found in this communion of persons. He writes:

> Man became the image and likeness of God not only through his own humanity, but also through the communion of persons which man and woman form right from the beginning… Man becomes the image of God not so much in the moment of solitude as in the moment of communion.[12]

Spousal meaning of the body
Without self-giving there can be no communion with others, and without communion the self remains locked in a prison of isolation, deprived of the joy of giving and receiving, loving and being loved. The image of God becomes manifest in the capacity of giving and receiving, of making that sincere gift of self to the other and establishing a communion of persons. Pope John Paul calls this capacity for self-giving "the spousal meaning of the body", and writes:

> The spousal meaning of the body includes from the beginning the spousal attribute, that is, the capacity of expressing love, that love in which the person becomes a gift and – by means of this gift – fulfils the meaning of his being and existence.[13]

The spousal meaning of the body is the most distinguishing human feature of what it means to be a man or woman. In creating humans, God inscribes in man and woman the capacity to be a gift to one another. Our communion "images" the divine communion,

---

12 Pope John Paul II, *Man and Woman He Created Them: A Theology of the Body*, 9:3.
13 As above, 15:1.

and men and women in their communion of persons mirror the trinitarian mystery of God. Their very bodies are the source of this image because through their bodies they have the capacity to enter into a communion of persons. The most tangible example of the gift of the self is the marital embrace, when conjugal union is established. But the gift of self is also made in friendship, and in a complete and total way in the celibate commitment of life in the service of God and people.

The spousal capacity of the body enables us to reach out to one another and make a sincere gift of self in marriage, friendship or celibate commitment to the Lord and the Church. That is true love. The opposite of true love is not hate, but using. If we use one another we reduce each other to the status of mere object. It is the most un-Godlike way of relating to another person. This refusal to love another person for his or her own sake is what we call sin, because it always includes the denial of the mystery of the divine indwelling in the other. On the human level it is a distortion of our greatest capacity. And it prevents us from discovering our true selves. That is why sin, the selfish act of putting self before and above others, always causes division.

Being made in the image of God means that we are created for a life of communion. We already have the capacity to enter into relationship with one another and establish a communion of persons through the sincere gift of self. God indwells this capacity. The God who dwells within us makes his home precisely in the heart which he has endowed with the capacity for living in union and communion with others. In every act of true love we simultaneously make the gift of self to the other and discover our true self. In the very act of love, of making that sincere gift of self, we discover our likeness to God who gives himself to us without reserve.

God is love. When we are acting as the image of God we are capable of loving in the way God loves. So, when Jesus says: "If anyone loves me... my Father will love him and we shall come to him and make our home with him" (John 14:24), he is saying that in the very act of loving him our hearts have become the image of God and the triune God can dwell within us. We become the temple of the living God. It is only when we see ourselves and others in the light of this amazing, revealed truth that we get to know ourselves as we truly are. And we shouldn't allow our sins and weaknesses to deflect our vision. Instead of becoming obsessed with our sinfulness we rejoice in the love and mercy and forgiveness of God as we turn to him in our hearts. We have been redeemed. We rejoice in our redemption.

Self before others: where does this tendency come from?

We could ask the question, and indeed every culture throughout history has asked this question, why is there this consistent tendency in human beings to put their own perceived egoistic goal before the common goal of humanity? Why do people seek fulfilment in individualism rather than in communion? Some say that within the evolutionary process we have not yet arrived at the stage of consciousness where we realise that it is only the common good that is truly the good of each individual. Some of those who take this view are hoping that the next stage of progress is to arrive at a more perfect state. And some take the Christian view and explain this basic selfishness in terms of original sin, that primeval Fall which is so dramatically symbolised in the story of Adam and Eve. While many Christians, including Christian scientists, take the evolutionary view, they also accept the biblical revelation of a "fall from grace". The effects of the Fall are all around and within us. So it is clear that there is some kind of moral or ethical war going on in the human heart, a war that St Paul summarised this way: "I do not do the good I want, but the evil I do not want is what I do" (Romans 7:19).

Are we dealing, then, with a failure of the evolutionary process to produce a human response to match the human ideal of love and peace with all, or are we dealing with something else – namely a deliberate failure on the part of the human to be fully human? However one answers that question – whether our response is atheistic, agnostic or theistic – we're still left with the human inclination to put the self first. Why are humans, who are capable of such love and self-sacrifice, also capable of such heartless cruelty and indifference to the plight of others? And, if natural selection weeds out, eventually, those characteristics that militate against the survival of the species, why has this tendency not been eliminated? Since it has the potential to destroy the whole world, for instance through nuclear weapons, the human race's very survival depends on it being eradicated. One would expect, then, that the process of natural selection would have dealt with it by now. But if this tendency is due to a failure in the spiritual order, a rupture of human relationship with God, then the natural selection process will not be capable of eradicating it. That can be done only by God. That is precisely what Christians believe.

We need the salvation or redemption that Christ brings. It is "the God within", and not the powerful process of natural selection, which redeems us from our brokenness. It is God, not science nor evolutionary theories or philosophies, who has the last word on what he has created. As Pope Benedict said:

> It is not science that redeems man: man is redeemed by love. This applies even in terms of this present world. When someone has the experience of a great love in his life, this is a moment of "redemption" which gives a new meaning to his life. But soon he will also realise that the love bestowed upon him cannot by itself resolve the question of his life. It is love that remains fragile. It can be destroyed by death. The human being needs unconditional love. He needs the certainty which makes him say: "neither death, nor life, nor angels, nor principalities nor things present, nor things to come, nor powers, nor height, nor depth, nor anything else in all creation, will be able to separate us from the love of

God in Christ Jesus our Lord" (Romans 8:38-39). If this absolute love exists, with its absolute certainty, then – only then – is man "redeemed", whatever should happen to him in his particular circumstances. This is what it means to say: Jesus Christ has "redeemed" us.[14]

Redeeming love

God comes to make his home in us. That is the astounding revelation that Jesus has given to us. This means that at the very centre of our being, an inexhaustible source of divine love resides. Regrettably we often keep a safe distance from that love. Indeed, our relationship with the God of love is often one of fear. How often does God have to tell us not to be afraid in the Bible? God reveals himself to us as love itself, and we often relate to him as if he were hostile. George Herbert caught this fear well in his poem:

> Love bade me welcome; yet my soul drew back,
> Guilty of dust and sin.
> But quick-ey'd Love, observing me grow slack
> From my first entrance in,
> Drew nearer to me, sweetly questioning,
> If I lack'd anything.

In the presence of totally giving and forgiving love the human spirit "draws back". We are unworthy; we are uncertain. Have we really got a right to enter that inner sanctuary of our heart where God dwells? That is the problem. It is one thing to believe that God dwells in heaven; it is quite another thing to believe that that same holy God dwells in our hearts. It is much easier to relate to God up in his heaven than to relate to God deep in our hearts. This problem can only be resolved by living faith. God has revealed to us that, through Christ, we have "our way to come to the Father" (Ephesians 2:18). As we pray in the Mass: "We thank you for counting us worthy

14 Pope Benedict XVI, *Spe Salvi* [Encyclical on Christian Hope] (London: Catholic Truth Society, 2007), 27.

to stand in your presence and serve you". By ourselves we have no right to come into God's presence; through Christ and in his Spirit we are invited and received into his presence.

The presence of the Holy Trinity in our hearts is the beginning here on earth of our eternal union with God in heaven. That divine presence within gives us a new perspective – a Christian perspective – on everything outside ourselves. It is the ground of all our hope. It is the knowledge of ourselves which enabled Paul to cry out: "For I am certain of this: neither death nor life, no angel, no prince, nothing that exists, nothing still to come, not any power, or height or depth, nor any created thing, can ever come between us and the love of God made visible in Christ Jesus our Lord" (Romans 8:38). If the creator of all dwells in our hearts the significance of every created thing is relative. Nothing created, no person, no thing, can become the final goal of a person's life. Our life and the "successes" of our life are ultimately judged by this indwelling presence of divine love, the Holy Trinity in our hearts, and not by external circumstances. Our hearts must be set on becoming one with the God within and not on external factors. Jesus said:

> Do not store up treasures for yourselves on earth, where moths and woodworms destroy them and thieves break in and steal. But store treasures for yourselves in heaven, where neither moth nor woodworms destroy them and thieves cannot break in and steal. For where your treasure is, there will your heart be also (Matthew 6:19).

As St Augustine said: "You have made us for yourself, O Lord, and our hearts will find no rest until they rest in you".[15] The God who made us, and for whom we exist, has made his home in our hearts. That is the source of our human dignity, the source of the deep joy that wells up in the heart once we acknowledge this divine indwelling. Even when we sin we do not lose that dignity. God is

---

15 St Augustine, *Confessions*, 1, 1.

ever ready to receive us back into a loving union with himself. He never withdraws his gifts and he never ceases to love us.

Self in God

In presenting this mystery of the indwelling presence of God in our hearts, scripture also presents the mystery in another way. God not only lives in us, but we also live in God. In his famous speech in Athens, Paul said that God is not far from anyone because: "it is in him that we live, and move, and exist" (Acts 17:28). And St John says: "Whoever keeps his commandments lives in God and God lives in him" (1 John 3:24). We live and move and have our being in God. But God shows his infinite love for us by living in us, by making us his temple, the home of his Son, Jesus Christ.

In the light of this revelation we might wonder where the self really exists? We have the answer in the Bible: it exists in God. We don't exist in a vacuum; nor do we simply exist in the visible, created world. Our very being is immersed in God, who is the source and the ground of all being. In the biblical perspective we have this extraordinary reciprocal indwelling – God dwelling in us and we in God. Paul struggled to express this revelation: "I live now not with my own life but with the life of Christ who lives in me" (Galatians 2:20).

The doctrine of the indwelling of the Holy Trinity in the human heart and in the heart of all creation is the foundation of all prayer. As Pope Benedict said: "The success of our lives is found in our participation in the trinitarian life offered to us".[16]

A confrère of mine gave an eloquent witness to God's abiding fidelity. Some years before he died he wrote:

> I was a laicised priest, dispensed from my religious vows. Although I had a good job I had never really come to terms with my new status as a lay Catholic. Years ago I had known the Lord at a fairly deep level but now it was almost as if he

---

16 Pope Benedict XVI, *Sacramentum Caritatsi* [The Sacrament of Charity], 2007, 94.

didn't exist. I barely went to Mass on Sunday, but that was all. No prayer. No sacraments for over five years. My faith seemed dead.

My mother died, and as the eldest son, I had to make all the funeral arrangements. The Requiem Mass was to take place at our local parish church. Family and friends would be there. I hadn't been to that church since I left the priesthood as I was too well known there. I went to Mass elsewhere so no one knew that I abstained from Holy Communion. I could hardly stay away from the funeral Mass, but what about Communion? Should I harden my heart, play the coward and make a bad Communion. I could never do that. Should I simply abstain? But this was my mother's funeral! How could I not enter into it fully? There was, of course, a third option: a good confession. That sent a shiver up my spine. Could I really go after all I'd done, after all these years? The prospect was not a little daunting. Could I even make a sincere confession? I felt profoundly disturbed. What I didn't realise was that the "Hound of Heaven" was at work. He wanted me to enter into myself. My faith was certainly not dead. But I felt so weak, so frightened.

Two days later I was walking down the road near my home when I had the most extraordinary experience. Suddenly, without any warning, I felt the Lord was very near. His presence was almost tangible. He was, as it were, bursting to enter my heart, making me an offer I couldn't refuse. The Lord I had once known and loved, the Lord who still loved me and had never stopped loving me! Did Saul feel like this on the road to Damascus? A kind of happiness flooded into my soul. Yes, I would make that confession come what may.

The evening before the funeral I went to Westminster Cathedral clutching my long list of mortal sins feeling dreadfully nervous and hoping the light in the confessional would be on so that I could read. It wasn't! I blurted out my confession as best I could, experiencing now what so many penitents feel and heard the beautiful words "I absolve you from your sins". "For your penance," the priest said, "receive Holy Communion at the Mass just beginning." "Is that all, Father?" "Yes. Go in peace." What was I trying to do? Pay for my sins? Didn't I know that they had already been paid for?

What did I feel as I left the confessional? Like someone emerging from a deep, dark dungeon into the warmth and brightness of a summer's day. I felt as if chains that had held me captive for so long were broken at last. I was FREE. Let no one ever convince you that Jesus didn't come to free the captive. That is not just figurative language. I know it is literally true because I was experiencing it. I had met the Lord. He had returned to re-establish a relationship that was deeper and more intense than ever before.

The Lord never does things by halves. In due course he gave me the incredible invitation to return to my religious congregation and the priesthood. He waited for my "Yes" or "No". There was to be no compulsion. Only I could give the answer and it had to be given freely. Naturally I hesitated. Would the congregation have me back? The Lord reassured me. Never did he let me feel like a second-class citizen. I was someone who was loved and wanted and valued. When I gave my "Yes" doors began to open, doors I had thought were shut for ever. But that is another story.

It's significant that his moment of grace came through the death of his mother. When he felt the Lord's presence, almost tangible, and "bursting" to enter his heart, those years in the wilderness were suddenly over. It all began with the inspiration to make a good confession. And as he entered into himself he discovered that the God whom he once knew and loved was waiting for him. Indeed, God had never left him. Through his personal experience of conversion, he learnt the truth that Christ had died for his sins, and that all he had to do was return, enter into himself and find God waiting to welcome him. Consequently he discovered a relationship that was deeper and more intense than ever before.

This work of the Holy Trinity is beautifully summed up by Paul, in his letter to the Ephesians:

> This, then, is what I pray, kneeling before the Father, from whom every family, whether spiritual or natural, takes its name:
>
> Out of his infinite glory, may he give you power through his Spirit for your hidden self to grow strong, so that Christ may live in your hearts through faith, and then, planted in love and built on love, you will with all the saints have strength to grasp the breadth and the length, the height and the depth; until, knowing the love of Christ, which is beyond all knowledge, you are filled with the utter fullness of God (3:14-19).

Through the gift of God our Father, the Holy Spirit strengthens us, renews our inner being, and Christ comes to dwell in our heart through faith. As Paul says in his first letter to the Corinthians: "Didn't you realise that you were God's temple and that the Spirit of God was living among you?" (3:16).

Personal spiritual exercise

- Centre yourself, using the techniques we learned in week one.
- Bring yourself to bodily stillness and calm.
- Now ask yourself: Do I really believe that God dwells in me? Do I believe that my very being is in God?
- Now be still.
- Now focus again on your breathing.
- And bring yourself gently back to the world.

10

Life in Abundance

Jesus described the purpose of his mission in this way: "I have come so that they may have life and have it to the full" (John 10:10). This fullness of life which Christ brings us is the gift of God our Father. As we pray in the third Eucharistic Prayer: "Father, you alone are holy and all creation rightly gives you praise. All life, all holiness comes from you through your Son, Jesus Christ our Lord, by the working of the Holy Spirit." God our Father is the creator of all life. Everything that is, from the greatest to the least, owes its being to the creative love of the Father. The Father of all life rejoices in the life he creates. Death was never part of his creative designs. As the scriptures assure us:

> Death was not God's doing,
> he takes no pleasure in the extinction of the living.
> To be – for this he created all; (Wisdom 1:13-14).
> Yet God did make man imperishable,
> he made him in the image of his own nature;
> it was the devil's envy that brought death into the world,
> as those who are his partners will discover (Wisdom 2:23-24).

Pope John Paul II, in his encyclical on the value and inviolability of human life (*Evangelium Vitae*) writes:

> The Gospel of life, proclaimed in the beginning when man was created in the image of God for a destiny of full and perfect life is contradicted by the painful experience of death which enters the world and casts its long shadow of meaninglessness over man's existence. Death came into the world as a result of the devil's envy and the sin of our first parents. And death entered it in a violent way, through the killing of Abel by his brother Cain.[1]

In the scriptures, God is clearly seen as the creator of life, while man, in the person of Cain, is the perpetrator of death. The destructive, anti-life consequences of the sin of Adam and Eve are visible in the envy and hatred in Cain's heart, which led him to murder his brother. Long before Abel suffered physical death at the hands of his brother, Cain had already suffered spiritual death.

This hostility to life, evidenced by envy, anger, enmity and ultimately murder, is the devil's work. The devil seeks to destroy what God has done. That is why St John says: "It was to undo all that the devil has done that the Son of God appeared" (1 John 3:8). The life which the devil set out to destroy was already created in, and through, and for Christ. The evil arrogance of the devil is clearly seen not just in his brother's murder, but in Cain's attempt to destroy the very gift of life itself, the gift which comes to us through Christ by the working of the Holy Spirit.

Jesus: true life

The Gospel of life is the Gospel of Jesus Christ because Jesus is, as he says: "the Way, the Truth and the Life" (John 14:6). When Jesus' distraught and grieving friend, Martha, tells him that she knows her brother would not have died if he had been there, Jesus responds:

---

1 *Evangelium Vitae*, 7.

"I am the resurrection. If anyone believes in me, even though he dies he will live, and whoever lives and believes in me will never die" (John 11:25-26). Pope John Paul II writes that this same life has been bestowed on us by the gift of the Spirit: "It is in being destined to life in its fullness, to 'eternal life', that every person's earthly life acquires its full meaning."[2] We were chosen for this life before the world came into being. This eternal choice of God, whereby each of us is known and chosen and loved, constitutes the very ground of our human dignity. St Gregory of Nyssa wrote:

> Man, as a being, is of no account; he is dust, grass, vanity. But once he is adopted by the God of the universe as a son, he becomes part of the family of that Being, whose excellence and greatness no one can see, hear or understand. What words, thoughts or flight of the spirit can praise the superabundance of this grace? Man surpasses his nature: mortal, he becomes eternal; human, he becomes divine.[3]

And because God adopts each person as his beloved son or daughter, God wants each one to live with his eternal life – to have life in abundance. Pope John Paul says:

> The life which God bestows upon man is much more than mere existence in time. It is a drive towards fullness of life; it is the seed of existence which transcends the very limits of time.[4]

So we have been created for everlasting life. Our response to God for this gift should always be one of one praise and gratitude, which the Holy Spirit teaches us to cultivate, by thanking God for the wonder of our own, unique self:

---

2 *Evangelium Vitae*, 80.

3 As above.

4 As above.

> It was you who created my inmost self,
> and put me together in my mother's womb;
> for all these mysteries I thank you:
> for the wonder of myself, for the wonder of your works
> (Psalm 139:13-14).

Spirituality of true self-esteem

Psalm 139 teaches us to thank God for the wonder of ourselves. The Hebrew scriptures also tell us that, despite our fallen state, we are made in the image and likeness of God (Genesis 1:26); "little less than a God" (Psalm 8:5); and precious in God's eyes (Isaiah 43:4). Furthermore, the New Testament tells us that our bodies are temples of the Holy Spirit (1 Corinthians 6:19). If these profound truths about ourselves find no resonance in how we see ourselves or, more fundamentally, how we feel about ourselves, they will very quickly become irrelevant and die. If, however, they find a home in our hearts, our response is one of grateful self-acceptance and self-esteem. Then we will begin to rejoice in the fullness of life that Christ gives us.

Pope John Paul II, in his very first encyclical, gave us a magnificent vision of true self-esteem:

> Those who wish to understand themselves thoroughly – and not just in accordance with the immediate, partial, often superficial, and even illusory standards and measures of their being – must with all their unrest, uncertainty and even their weakness and sinfulness, with their life and death, draw near to Christ. They must, so to speak, enter into him with their own self, they must "appropriate" and assimilate the whole reality of the Incarnation and the Redemption in order to find themselves. If this profound process takes place within them, they then bear fruit not only in adoration of God but also of deep wonder at themselves.[5]

---

5 *Redemptor Hominis*, 10.

Deep wonder at ourselves and our creation is the fruit of faith. Who can begin to imagine the dignity that we have as sons and daughters of God? Pope John Paul dares to imagine it with this very arresting statement:

> In reality, the name for that deep amazement at man's worth and dignity is the Gospel, that is to say: the Good News. It is also called Christianity. This amazement determines the Church's mission in the world and, perhaps even more so "in the modern world".[6]

The Gospel is not just about God and his mercy for us. The Gospel is about human dignity, about our worth as the children of God. Jesus came to give us "life in abundance" because God loved us. Our greatest challenge is to connect what we believe about God, with what we believe about ourselves. Paul knew how to do it – without a blush he can say: "We are God's work of art, created in Christ Jesus" (Ephesians 2:10). Believing in God our creator means that we believe in ourselves as God's work of art. If we believe this, and if we live by every word that comes from the mouth of God (Matthew 4:4), then we have every reason to experience the deep joy of being blessed and loved by God. Indeed, failure to cultivate true self-esteem is a denial of God's word.

In my book *The Inside Job: A Spirituality of True Self-Esteem*,[7] I tried to show how self-esteem begins with obeying Jesus' command to live by every word that comes from the mouth of God. Why should we open our hearts to the negative or destructive things that people sometimes say about us, while resisting or only half believing what God says? It is God's revelation to us about ourselves, rather than the negative comments of other people, that should shape and determine how we see ourselves.

6 *Redemptor Hominis*, 10.

7 Jim McManus C.Ss.R., *The Inside Job: A Spirituality of True Self-Esteem* (Chawton: Redemptorist Publications, 2005).

We can identify this process at work in our spirituality. True self-knowledge leads to true self-esteem. True awareness of who we are in Christ – namely God's work of art – protects us from the sinful negativity that can be all around and within us. We may say: "Your word, O Lord, is spirit and it is life", but then go on to live by what our negative critics – both external and internal – tell us. But it's possible to live by the life-giving word of God, even when we're surrounded by the noise of negativity. And why shouldn't we rejoice when God tells us that we are his work of art? Should we not sing, with Mary: "The Almighty has done great things for me" (Luke 1:49) instead of joining in a chorus of self-denigration? We get it right at Mass when we say in the second Eucharistic Prayer: "We thank you for counting us worthy to stand in your presence and serve you". When we do so, we are standing in good self-esteem before God. We also get it right when we pray in the third Eucharistic Prayer: "May he make us an everlasting gift to you". That is good self-esteem – when we see that, despite all our sin, Jesus makes us an everlasting gift to God.

Harmonising the way we see ourselves with the way we pray about ourselves in the liturgy is not an illusionary ground for self-esteem. Rather, it is seeing ourselves as God sees us. I like to put this challenge to people, especially to those who are cynical on the subject: God tells you that you are in his own image and likeness, precious in his sight, the temple of his Holy Spirit, a work of art. If that is not how you see yourself, who has got it right? You or God? As the Second Vatican Council said:

> In reality it is only in the mystery of the Word made flesh that the mystery of humanity truly becomes clear… Christ, the new Adam, in the very revelation of the mystery of the Father and of his love, fully reveals humanity to itself and brings to light its very high calling.[8]

---

8 *Gaudium et Spes*, 22.

If we do not know ourselves as Christ does, we haven't yet got to know ourselves. Christ reveals us to ourselves, so Christian formation should enable us to evaluate ourselves in the light of this revelation. But sadly, as Jesuit psychiatrist Fr Jim Gill points out: "People evaluate their personal worth not so much by looking at themselves as by measuring their success".[9] Christ's revelation makes no difference to this evaluation.

This acceptance of the self is not just of my soul – the "spiritual" part of me – it is acceptance of my totality, both spiritual and physical. In a special way, it is acceptance of my body. As Pope John Paul II writes:

> The human body, and only the body, is capable of making visible what is invisible: the spiritual and the divine. It was created to transfer into the visible reality of the world the mystery hidden from eternity in God, and thus to be a sign of it.[10]

Pope John Paul sees the human body as a sacrament, the means God uses to make visible his own invisible nature. Pope Benedict XVI has also written about how the body is regarded in Christian spirituality:

> Nowadays, Christianity of the past is often criticised as being opposed to the body, and it is quite true that tendencies of this sort have always existed. Yet the contemporary way of exalting the body is deceptive. Eros, reduced to pure sex, has become a commodity, a mere "thing" to be bought and sold, or rather, man himself becomes a commodity. This is hardly man's great "yes" to the body. On the contrary, he now considers his body and his sexuality as the purely material part of himself, to be used... as a mere object that he attempts, as he pleases, to make both enjoyable and harmless.[11]

---

9 Jim Gill, *Human Development*, no 3 (1980), 34.

10 Pope John Paul II, *Man and Woman He Created Them: A Theology of the Body*, 19:4.

11 *Deus Caritas Est*, 5.

Negativity towards the body goes hand in hand with cynicism towards the self, an unconscious denial of Christ's gift of abundant life. There is a common assumption that we can't have any self-esteem, given the sinful, weak and corrupt nature of our bodies. It is a far cry from Paul's words of encouragement:

> Your body, you know, is the temple of the Holy Spirit, who is in you since you received him from God. You are not your own property; you have been bought and paid for. That is why you should use your body for the glory of God (1 Corinthians 6:19-20).

That is surely a very good reason for accepting our bodies, no matter what shape or size or age and no matter how weak. As Pope John Paul said: "In reality, the name for that deep amazement at man's worth and dignity is the Gospel".[12] But it can take years to integrate this vision into our whole approach to spirituality.

We can set out on the path to self-esteem using the words of the Psalm: "I thank you: for the wonder of myself" (Psalm 139.14). My relationship with myself shapes and controls every other relationship in my life. If I am engaging in some form of subtle self-rejection; if I refuse to accept myself as I am – perhaps because I am not as clever, or as rich, or as successful as I would like to be – I will find it very hard to experience the love and acceptance of others. Self-rejection is the painful road that leads to anger and disappointment with ourselves, and to jealousy and negative attitudes towards others. It is not the same as humility. It is an inner wound that often leads us to seek comfort in pride, whereas self-esteem rejoices in self-acceptance. In fact pride is the very opposite of self-esteem, because it operates through invidious comparison. But if we accept ourselves just as we are, we have no need to ever compare ourselves with anyone else.

---

12 *Redemptor Hominis*, 10.

In order to cultivate this gratitude for ourselves we need to foster what Pope John Paul II calls "a contemplative outlook". This, he writes, is:

> ... the outlook of those who see life in its deeper meaning, who grasp its utter gratuitousness, its beauty and its invitation to freedom and responsibility. It is the outlook of those who do not presume to take possession of reality but instead accept it as a gift, discovering in all things the reflection of the creator and seeing in every person his living image.[13]

Because God, not man, is the author of life, life is always a gift; never a commodity, or something for us to dispose of as we will. And the gift of the fullness of life should evoke a response full of gratitude. But the most horrendous crimes take place when life is treated as a commodity. When rulers see life as a commodity, the very security of the human race is undermined: conflicts which should be settled by talking lead to wars, and human life is sacrificed in the furtherance of some political ambition. Often, the dignity of human life is sacrificed on the altar of economic greed: in the name of modernisation and economic efficiency, hundreds of thousands of people are thrown out of work. A few people make huge profits, while many others endure hardship and unemployment.

Similarly, when couples see life as a commodity rather than a divine gift, avoiding some perceived disadvantage to themselves or their family can take precedence over the joy of created life, and abortion is often justified in terms of economic or social or eugenic efficiency. When life is seen as a commodity, the debility, suffering and loneliness of old age will be brought to an end by induced death under the name of euthanasia. In fact, when life is seen as a commodity, only "high-quality" life – measured on a scale of health, wealth and success – is regarded as worthwhile. The unborn and the old, the disabled and terminally ill, are all at risk. Death,

---

13 *Evangelium Vitae*, 80.

and not life in abundance, becomes the objective and a culture of death, rather than life, prevails.

So many good people are misled by fallacious moral principles. If there is no objective truth about what is right and wrong, people will ultimately judge everything by the impact it has on themselves. If it is helpful and convenient, it will be declared good in itself; if it is unhelpful or inconvenient, it will be declared bad. Jesus' answer to the man who asked: "Master, what good deed must I do to possess eternal life?" (Matthew 19:16) is God's word to each of us: "Why do you ask me about what is good? There is one alone who is good. But if you wish to enter into life, keep the commandments" (verse 17). God's commandments are his life-giving word. As scripture says: "The law of the Lord is perfect, reviving the soul" (Psalm 19:7). To have within us the fullness of life, we must live in accordance with the life-giving word of God. This word is faithfully handed on to us by the Church which, as Paul said, "upholds the truth and keeps it safe" (1 Timothy 3:15). As the Vatican Council said:

> The task of authentically interpreting the word of God, whether in its written form or in that of tradition, has been entrusted only to those charged with the Church's living Magisterium, whose authority is exercised in the name of Jesus Christ.[14]

We should never be surprised if our Christian teaching on life is unacceptable to the world around us. If we have to choose between what the papers say and what the Church says, we have made that choice a long time ago. We made it when we said in the Creed: "We believe in the one, holy, catholic and apostolic Church". In the words of Cardinal Newman's hymn:

> And I hold in veneration
> for the love of him alone
> Holy Church as his creation
> and her teaching as his own.

---

14 *Dei Verbum*, 10.

The abundant life which Jesus came to give us begins with the gift of our physical life. That gift is sacred. But it takes on a whole new dimension when God fills the person he has created with his own divine life. Jesus spoke about this in terms of rebirth:

> I tell you most solemnly,
> unless a man is born through water and the Spirit,
> he cannot enter the kingdom of God:
> what is born of the flesh is flesh;
> what is born of the Spirit is spirit (John 3:5-6).

God creates not just our physical life; he also shares with us his own eternal life, making us his adopted sons and daughters. The very purpose and meaning of our life on earth is to live gratefully in the full consciousness of who we are as children of God. St John encourages us to do that: "Think of the love that the Father has lavished on us, by letting us be called God's children; and that is what we are" (1 John 3:1). When we think about this love, we begin to develop a contemplative focus, and our perspectives begin to change. Things which may have formerly loomed large begin to take their proper place. Damian and Cathy Stayne, a young married couple, share how their perspectives on life changed when they opened themselves to the new and abundant life of Christ:

> We both come from Catholic families with deep faith, both sets of parents were active members of the church, locally and nationally. As young people we walked away from many of the values held by our parents and experienced, as a result, the confusion and pain that accompanies setting one's heart on things of this world and seeking fulfilment and meaning in temporal things. Having tasted the fruitlessness of pursuing life without God at the centre we both then had powerful adult conversion experiences, through involvement in the Catholic Charismatic Renewal. This gave us a new joy and a desire to live for God.

We first met each other at the South London Chaplaincy and got married five years later. We now lead a Catholic Charismatic Community called Cor Lumen Christi (The Heart and Light of Christ) which has forty-five members living various expressions of commitment on both a residential and non-residential basis. Our shared life involves evangelistic outreach, works of mercy, the simplification of our lifestyles, teaching, training, formation, the celebration of the sacraments, praise, worship, adoration and a deep life of prayer.

Living life closely with others who have also chosen to live for God before all else is extremely encouraging, challenging and rewarding. It empowers us to live a more radical Gospel lifestyle than might otherwise be possible for us on our own. It dismantles our facades and false "personas", demanding that the real person emerge and thus releases us to become more and more ourselves, which is actually a great relief. Deep communion is not possible between "personas", only between real people. We have discovered that love can only be genuine when we are genuinely ourselves. We have found that a deeper love and freedom are now possible and life is far less superficial. The effect of this on our spiritual lives is to bring deeper reality and vulnerability into our relationship with God enabling us to more deeply "receive the Holy Spirit" (John 20:22), and believe ourselves loved just as we are. This, in turn, brings greater peace and joy.

Life in the spirit in community is for us a full life which calls forth the gifts of its members. We experience a more healthy interdependence through our shared life and mission and each one has his or her role and part to play. We are highly motivated because we know that what we do has eternal consequences and that we can play a significant part in God's plan. The committed friendships and support we enjoy increase our effectiveness because we know we are all pulling together for a common purpose. While we recognise things are by no means perfect, we feel we do live a life that is very worthwhile, in which we are growing in God.

We now know that all we were searching for can be found in a life of deep communion with God. It is, we have discovered, a profound experience of this divine communion that is the longing of every human heart. We believe that the call to community is a strategy of the Holy Spirit to help people to enter into divine communion as a way of life and thus share in God's own experience of abundant life.

Through their conversion, Damian and Cathy received the grace to seek God and the kingdom of God before all other things. They began to live by the word of Jesus: "Set your hearts on his kingdom first, and on his righteousness, and all these other things will be given you as well" (Matthew 6:33). So it was through conversion that they began to experience abundant life. And in return, God has *hallowed his name* in Damian and Cathy, and in the community of young men and women they lead.

Personal spiritual exercise

- Centre yourself, using the techniques we learned in week one.
- Bring yourself to bodily stillness and calm.
- Now ask yourself: Am I ready to receive the abundant life that Jesus wants to give me? Am I willing to let go of anything in my life that is opposed to this abundant life?
- Now be still.
- Now focus again on your breathing.
- And bring yourself gently back to the world.

11

✢ Finding God in All Things ✢

The Psalmist sings: "As a deer longs for flowing streams, so my soul longs for you, O God" (Psalm 42:1). The deepest yearning in the human heart, though we may not always recognise it, is for God. As St Augustine said: "You have made us for yourself, O Lord, and our hearts will find no rest until they rest in you."[1] Our goal, the end and purpose of our life, is union with God. The desire for this union keeps our hearts searching, restless, yearning. This desire will only be perfectly satisfied in heaven. But this desire is not just for that perfect union with God in heaven. God invites us, here and now, in this world, to live in union with him. He invites us to live in his presence; to listen to his voice, speak to him, serve him and, most of all, to love him with our whole heart. God invites us to pray, "Let my heart rejoice in your saving help" (Psalm 13:5). Joy is the beautiful fruit of the Spirit which the Lord wants us to have in our hearts at all times, even when times are difficult. Joy, flowing from the truth of who we are as God's beloved, sustains us in all circumstances. Joy, as St Augustine said, flows from truth:

---

1 St Augustine, *Confessions*, 1, 1.

> That is the authentic happy life, to set one's joy on you, grounded in you and caused by you... The happy life is joy based on the truth. This is joy grounded in you, O God, who are the truth.[2]

And the truth that God has revealed to us is that he is with us always and that we will be with him for ever.

God wills us to live in union with him, not just when we pray or go to church, but at all times and in all places. Because God is as truly present in the factory as in the church; as really present in our daily work as in our daily prayer. God is absent from nothing. In fact, if God were absent we would literally have no thing, nothing, because no thing could exist without God. Pope John Paul II wrote in his encyclical, *Faith and Reason*: "God comes to us in the things we know best and can verify most easily, the things of our everyday life, apart from which we cannot understand ourselves."[3]

A holistic spirituality finds God in the familiar things of life, the things that we most love, such as family and friends. We find God in our work and our leisure. But if we are not also consciously giving time to God in prayer, it is more difficult to find God in all things. We have to be contemplatives in action – seeing the face of God in the depths of our being; contemplatives in action – finding God in the very busyness of our life.

The Vatican Council encouraged a whole new spirituality for the laity, a spirituality of the marketplace, where God is truly present:

> By reason of their special vocation it belongs to the laity to seek the kingdom of God by engaging in temporal affairs and directing them according to God's will. They live in the world, that is, they are engaged in each and every work and business of the earth and in the ordinary circumstances of social and family life, which, as it were, constitute their very existence.[4]

---

2 St Augustine, *Confessions*, 10, 23.

3 Pope John Paul II, *Fides et Ratio*, 12.

4 *Lumen Gentium*, 31.

From these situations and activities which constitute the very existence of the vast majority of the Church, namely the laity, God is not absent. At times, in the past, regrettably, the laity was given the impression that only those who "left the world" for the priesthood or religious life were on the high road to heaven. In fact, this very insidious distinction was introduced into theology: religious were called to holiness by following the way of the evangelical counsels – namely the three vows of poverty, chastity and obedience – while the laity was called to salvation by following the way of the ten commandments. The Vatican Council officially ruled out such a spurious distinction, and in his time Pope John Paul frequently reaffirmed the Council's teaching:

> The vocation of the lay faithful to holiness implies that life according to the Spirit expresses itself in a particular way in their involvement in temporal affairs and in their participation in earthly activities. Once again the apostle admonishes us: "whatever you do, in word or deed, do everything in the name of the Lord Jesus, giving thanks to God the Father through him" (Colossians 3:17). Applying the apostle's words to the lay faithful, the Council categorically affirms: neither family concerns nor other secular affairs should be excluded from their religious programme of life.[5]

Working in the midst of the world is not an obstacle to holiness, because God is as present in the noise of the busy world as he is in the silence of a monastery. The God who is present to the monk in silence and prayer is equally present to the labourer in the fields or in the factory. The Vatican Council stated:

> One of the gravest errors of our time is the dichotomy between the faith which many profess and the practice of their daily lives... Let there be no such pernicious opposition

---

5 *Apostolic Exhortation on the Vocation of the Laity*, 17.

between professional and social activity on the one hand and religious life on the other. The Christian who shirks his temporal duties shirks his duties to his neighbour, neglects God himself, and endangers his eternal salvation.[6]

The Church clearly teaches the good news that our life is not compartmentalised into the secular and the spiritual, into daily work and daily prayer, into action and contemplation. Our life is a unity. The secret for integrating the secular and the spiritual is finding God in all things. This requires training of heart and spirit.

Practical Steps

Each of us has a capacity for contemplation. We can look in wonder at beautiful things; we can be deeply moved by human joy or sorrow; we can be still and silent in the presence of loved ones. In each of these emotions the deepest reality we experience is the presence of God. But so often we haven't woken up to that presence. The real difference between the contemplative and the non-contemplative is like the difference between a person who is fast asleep and a person who is enjoying his work. The sleeping person is totally unaware of the world around him. Too often, our bodies are wide awake, taking part in all kinds of activities, full of human interest – but our spirits are asleep, only vaguely aware of the life within and around us. Within us, God is present – loving and sustaining us, and inviting us to a life of communion. God is present in each event and in each situation, so we need to waken up to his presence.

The poet and patriot Joseph Mary Plunkett, who was executed for his part in the 1916 Easter Rising in Dublin, was wide awake to God's presence in the world. His poem on this divine presence is well known:

> I see his blood upon the rose
> And in the stars the glory of his eyes,

---

6 *Gaudium et Spes*, 43.

His body gleams amid eternal snows,
His tears fall from the skies.

I see his face in every flower;
The thunder and the singing of the birds
are but his voice – and carven by his power
Rocks are his written words.

All pathways by his feet are worn,
His strong heart stirs the ever-beating sea,
His crown of thorns is twined with every thorn,
His cross is every tree.

That is the contemplative spirit awake to the presence of God in all things. St Alphonsus Liguori, writing in eighteenth-century Italy, gave practical advice on this kind of prayer:

> When your eye rests on scenes in the country or along the shore, on flowers or fruits, and you are delighted by the sight and the scent of all, say, "Behold, how many are the beautiful creatures that God has created for me in this world that I may love him; and what further enjoyments does he not keep prepared for me in paradise."[7]

Sometimes we may find it easier to rejoice in God's presence when we behold some beautiful scene, than to see Christ really present in another person. Yet we believe Jesus when he tells us that whatever we do for the least of his brethren, we do for him (Matthew 25:40). Each person we encounter is a walking shrine of God's presence, a living tabernacle of Christ. We may only see an enemy, or a drunk, or a beggar, or a layabout. But as the Vatican Council said: "By his incarnation, he, the Son of God, has in a certain way united himself

---

7 Cited in Hoegerl, *Heart Calls to Heart*, 219.

with each individual."[8] Faith is like borrowing the eyes of Jesus. We start to cultivate finding God in all things when we look where he truly is – in other people, including people we live and work with, and even those with whom we have great trouble and conflict. If Christ is not in my enemy, by the same token, he is not in my friend! That is the challenge of the Gospel of Christ, that "amazement at human dignity" on which we have reflected throughout this book.

If we want to grow in this spirituality of finding God in all things we need to discipline our heart and mind so that our spirit stays awake. This is the importance of morning prayer. As we wake up to the new day we should wake up our spirit to the presence of God. You may say that morning is not your best time, but you don't have to make eloquent speeches to God. All you have to do is to acknowledge his presence, thank him for the new day, and offer him all your thoughts, words and actions of the day. It makes no difference if you are still sleepy. A sleepy morning offering will have the same effect on your spirit as a chirpy one! As we thank God for the gift of the new day we should remind ourselves that this is not just another twenty-four hours. This day is new because it is a brand new creation. It has never been here before and it would not be here now if God wasn't calling it into being.

The simple prayer of grace before meals can teach us a great deal about how to find God in all things. You have just prepared a meal, or someone has prepared a meal for you, and you sit down to enjoy it. You say "bless us, O Lord, and these thy gifts, which we are about to receive from your bounty, through Christ the Lord." In this prayer we acknowledge that it is all from God. God was in the shopping, the preparation, the cooking and the enjoying. And a simple grace is an appropriate prayer before any work. As I begin to type this page I can say, "Bless us, O Lord, and these thy gifts." And as I think about the chapter which I have just finished I can say, "We give thee thanks, O almighty God, for all thy benefits". God is present in all things. Prayer is like waking up to his presence. By

---

8 *Gaudium et Spes*, 22.

staying awake in his presence we are able to find him in all things. We become contemplatives in action.

Contemplative Prayer

Contemplative prayer is rooted in the grace of baptism, through which we are joined to Christ in the mystery of his union with the Father and the Holy Spirit. It is a gift of God. Centring prayer, or the technique of centring prayer, is the means by which we can prepare ourselves to be open to this gift of contemplation.

The doctrine of the indwelling of the Holy Trinity in the human heart and in the heart of all creation is the foundation of all prayer. As Pope Benedict XVI said: "The success of our lives is found in our participation in the trinitarian life offered to us".[9] The fullness of life is not found in outward success, no matter how magnificent, but in the growing awareness of the unconditional worth, dignity and utter uniqueness of one's own personal life. For the dawning of this awareness we need to enter into ourselves, into the depths of our heart, to be alone with ourselves and to find God in the depth of our being. So often we are tempted to seek God outside ourselves, as far away as possible from ourselves. St Augustine, after his discovery of God in the depths of his being, wrote with utter conviction:

> You are more intimately present to me than my inmost being and higher than the highest element in me... You were in front of me, but I, instead, had gone far from myself and could not find myself again, and even less could I find you again.[10]

Throughout the rest of his life Augustine kept the fire of his experience of God aflame. His example and teaching have shaped the spirituality of millions and encouraged generations of Christians to enter into their inmost hearts and find the consoling

---

9 *Sacramentum Caritatis*, 94.

10 Augustine, *Confessions*, 5, 2:2.

and redeeming presence of God there. God is not far from anyone. As St Paul said to the Athenians, it is in God that we "live, and move, and exist" (Acts 17:28). Or, as St John said: "God is love and anyone who lives in love lives in God, and God lives in him" (1 John 4:16).

If we want to find God we enter into the depth of our own heart. Heart, of course, does not refer to the physical organ, but to that immense inner world that is our spiritual depth. Each of us can withdraw into our own inner world and discover an immense universe of love and compassion, friendship and joy, as well as pain and rejection, fear and sadness, and maybe selfishness, bitterness and unforgiveness. When our heart becomes cluttered with negativity and sinfulness, when we become fixated in our hearts on our own plans and comforts, God offers us an extraordinary grace: "I shall give you a new heart, and put a new spirit in you; I shall remove the heart of stone from your bodies and give you a heart of flesh instead" (Ezekiel 36:26). God gives us the ability to transcend self, even as we enter to the depth of ourselves, and to find a new peace in our relationship with God and others. It is in this invisible universe within us, and not the visible world without, that God has made home. But as we enter into our hearts we must be open to encounter more than ourselves. As one writer points out:

> The important thing here is to realise that my depth is deeper than I am. But at the same time I may plunge into myself and never find anything more than myself. The self, in fact, is so deep that it can engulf me without my ever realising there is something further. It is easy to see why so many mystics lose themselves in themselves and never meet God.[11]

We have to be on our guard, then, against two pitfalls. On the one hand we have to avoid the trap of never entering into our deep heart and living only on the surface of life. On the other hand,

---

11 Egan, *Christian Mysticism*, 249.

we have to avoid blindly entering into the deep heart and missing all the signs of divine presence, deaf to the invitations that God extends to us. Those invitations are always the same: to love and patience, forgiveness and repentance, fuller growth in maturity and responsibility. It is only in the depths of our hearts, where God loves to dwell, that we can hear those divine invitations. God invites us to grow by gently reminding us of our true identity: "I have made you in my own image and likeness and I give you the capacity to become like me in what you do or say." Hearing this invitation empowers us to begin to live in a more "godlike" way as soon as we accept it. The invitation is always extended but our sinfulness often prevents us from accepting.

We have to be very pragmatic about the authenticity of our inward journey. If we are truly entering into our deep heart we will begin to see new fruit in our own lives. First of all we will begin to notice that we can accept ourselves, just as we are, in an unconditional way, and that this motivates us to ever deeper love and generosity. This love, in its turn, enables us to go beyond and transcend self and make the sincere gift of self to others. An experience of the deep heart that would turn us inwards, in selfish pre-occupation, would not be authentic; it would be a form of pseudo-mysticism.

Cultivating an awareness of God's presence in our hearts is what we mean by contemplation. To become aware of God's presence and live in that awareness, even for a minute, is the grace of contemplation. God is, as it were, waiting at the core of our being for us to respond to him. St Bernard gives us a very clear teaching on contemplation:

> The first step in contemplation is to consider what God wants, what is pleasing to him, what is acceptable in his sight. And since we all make many mistakes and the boldness of our will revolts against the rightness of his, and since the two cannot be brought into agreement and made to fit together, let us humble ourselves under the mighty hand of the most high

God. In the sight of his mercy, let us take pains to show how in all things we stand in need of his mercy, saying: "Heal me. O Lord, and I shall be healed; save me and I shall be saved", and "O Lord, be gracious to me; heal me, for I have sinned against you". Once the eye of the heart has been cleansed by dwelling on thoughts of this kind we are no longer left in bitterness in our own spirit, but we have a great joy in the Spirit of God. We do not now consider what is God's will for us, but what God's will is, in itself. Life is in his will.[12]

God in troubled times

After a healing service in which I had been leading a parish community in prayers of thanksgiving for God's holy and hidden presence in all the trouble and tragedies of life, a family of six waited for me – both parents, two sons and two daughters. They were all crying. I thought I might have upset them by something I said. "Oh no", the mother said, "our sixteen year old daughter was raped and murdered a year ago today and now we know that she wasn't all alone. Christ was with her." Their greatest pain came from the thought of their beautiful daughter all alone as her assassin brutalised and killed her. As they began to acknowledge the presence of God they received the grace to see that, despite the awful crime and their terrible loss, God was present. They were able to surrender their horror at her being all alone to God. They didn't ask, "Why didn't God stop the murderer?" That can be such a stumbling block. We believe that God is all loving and all powerful. Then why doesn't he stop wars, save the innocent, prevent disasters like earthquakes? Our Blessed Lady could have asked that at the foot of the cross. Christ's enemies did: "As for the leaders, they jeered at him. 'He saved others,' they said 'let him save himself if he is the Christ of God, the Chosen One'" (Luke 23:35).

St Paul faced this agonising question: where is God when evil things happen? He wrote:

---

12 Office of Readings, Wednesday, Week 23.

With God on our side who can be against us? Since God did not spare his own Son, but gave him up to benefit us all, we may be certain, after such a gift, that he will not refuse us anything he can give… Nothing therefore can come between us and the love of Christ, even if we are troubled or worried, or being persecuted, or lacking food and clothes, or being threatened or even attacked. As scripture promised: "For your sake we are being massacred daily, and reckoned as sheep for the slaughter." These are the trials through which we triumph, by the power of him loves us (Romans 8:31-33. 35-37).

To the person without faith Paul's answer is no answer; to the person with living faith no further answer is needed. I believe that grieving family had living faith. If the all-powerful Father didn't stop his Son from being nailed to the cross they were not going to ask him why he didn't stop their daughter being murdered. St Alphonsus Liguori, a man who knew great trouble in his own life, wrote:

When, therefore, you are afflicted with a sickness, temptation, persecution, or other trouble, go at once and ask him that his hand may help you. It is enough for you to present your affliction to him: to come in and say, "Look, O Lord, upon my distress" (Lamentations 1:20). He will not fail to comfort you, or at least to give you strength to suffer that grief with patience; and it will turn out a greater good to you than if you were already freed from it. Tell him all the thoughts of fear or of sadness that torment you and say to him, "My God in you are all my hopes; I offer you this affliction and resign myself to your will; but do you take pity on me – either deliver me out of it, or give me the strength to bear it".[13]

St Alphonsus knew from his own experience that in time of trouble fine theories are of little avail. We need living faith which enables

---

13 Hoegerl, *Heart Calls to Heart*, 257.

us to reach out to God and ask for help. At such times we can better understand the meaning of Jesus' words: "Unless you change and become like little children you will never enter the kingdom of heaven" (Matthew 18:3). In time of need the child cries out to its mother or father. In themselves, trouble or grief are bad enough; but when we exclude God and fail to cry for help like little children, they become unbearable. That is why St Paul encouraged the early Christians not to grieve about the dead "like the other people who have no hope" (1 Thessalonians 4:13). Paul is saying grieve by all means, but grieve with hope in the resurrection. The immediate pain of loss will be the same, but the assurance in faith will bring comfort and consolation in due course.

Lamentation

A mysticism of lamentation is a most pragmatic way for coping with times of trouble. One third of all the Psalms are prayers of lament to God about suffering and injustice. But there is an enormous difference between lamenting to God about bad things, and just lamenting. When we lament to God we know he is listening. Our isolation is overcome at the deepest level; the loneliness of inner distress is replaced by solidarity with God – with Jesus in his death on the cross – and we begin to experience companionship on our road of sorrow. The cause of the pain, suffering and distress may persist, but it loses its power to isolate us as we make our way along the *via dolorosa* – the way of sorrow.

Christians throughout the centuries have known the presence of Mary, the mother of Jesus, when they have found themselves on the road of sorrow. The road to Calvary was the most painful road one could imagine for any mother; standing at the foot of the cross was the most excruciating vigil a mother could keep. Yet Mary walked that road and kept that vigil without doubting that "the promise made to her by the Lord would be fulfilled" (Luke 1:45). Here we see the empowering and transforming power of faith. On the third day Mary saw her crucified Son, risen and glorified. At the end of every road to Calvary there is hope of resurrection. But notice that Mary had to walk that journey. Her faith was not an evasion. It was her very faith and love which brought her to walk that sorrowful journey. And she retained her contemplative silence as she heard the chief priests and scribes mock her son. And out of the evil of the crucifixion, God brought the new life of the resurrection.

Living in the present

Our challenge is to live fully aware of where we have come from, and alive to the possibilities which lie ahead. Having faced the final reality that lies ahead of each of us – namely death – we can then focus on how best to live our lives to the full. In 1936, Bartolome Marquez was only twenty-one years old when he was executed by the communist regime in Spain, for upholding his Catholic faith. The day before his death he wrote a remarkable letter to his girlfriend, Maruja.

> I look death in the eye and, believe my words, it does not daunt me or make me afraid. My sentence before the court of mankind will be my soundest defence before God's court; in their effort to revile me, they have ennobled me; in trying to sentence me, they have absolved me, and in attempting to lose me, they have saved me. Do you know what I mean? Why, of course! Because in killing me, they grant me true life and in condemning me for always upholding the highest ideals of religion, country, and family, they swing open before me the doors of heaven…[14]

The youthful writer of this beautiful testimony of faith in God and love for his girlfriend has been beatified by the Church and is now revered as Blessed Bartolome Marquez. He died a martyr's death. But the day before he died he lived intensely in the present moment.

Facing the reality of death doesn't mean becoming fixated or obsessed with it. But it does mean that we're able to live in the

---

14 Cited by Paul Murray OP, *Spirituality*, vol. 14, September-October 2008, 314.

present, free from those strategies of denial which only serve to create fear. Catholics pray the Hail Mary all their lives. It concludes with the words: "Pray for us now and at the hour of our death." Even in the most joyful moment of celebration, such as when we're thanking God for a newly married couple or a new baby, we effortlessly remind ourselves of the hour of our death. That is not a morbid preoccupation, but a healthy, realistic acceptance that our life in this world will come to an end. In every Mass we speak about our death in this way: "We are waiting in joyful hope for the coming of our Saviour, Jesus Christ." And we exclaim at Mass: "Christ has died, Christ is risen, Christ will come again." That is our faith and we profess it as we say during Mass: "We believe in the resurrection of the body and the life of the world to come".

Living in God's time

The Greek New Testament has two words for time: *chronos* – clock time or twenty-four-hour time; and *kairos* – God's time, the moment of grace, the hour of salvation. Within every moment of *chronos* there is a *kairos*, and the challenge is to find within the daytime or night time of our lives, the time of grace and salvation. It involves a shift of attitude towards how we see time. We have been accustomed to using time to get things done; now we seek, not to use time, but to find within time God's presence and grace. That is the contemplative attitude towards time.

"Time is money," says the businessman; "Time is where I find God's presence," says the contemplative. Living time as *kairos*, as a gift from God, opens up the whole contemplative dimension. At the heart of time as *chronos* there is shortage, a sense of the sands of time running out. But at he heart of time as *kairos* there is abundance, a sense of fulfilment, of today being the day that the Lord has made. Denial of death involves living simply in *chronos*. Not only that, living in denial of death robs the present moment of its depth, namely the moment when we are invited to find God's mercy and love. A healthy spirituality should be a constant critique of how we are coping with time and a constant reminder that when the cares and worries of *chronos* begin to mount up, we can dive into the ocean of *kairos* where we can unload all our worries onto the Lord.

Coping with loss is one of the big challenges of growing old. It's when people have to cope, not only with the physical process of aging, but also with the loss of others. You'll often hear extended family members say that they only meet at funerals. Older people also have to cope with giving up their professional life, along with all the financial benefits and relationships that go with it. One retiree put it succinctly when he said, "The free time I looked forward to enjoying was empty and I made many false move in trying to fill it."[15] But, as Judith Viorst said, "It is our attitude toward losses as much as the nature of our losses which will determine the quality of our old age."[16] A good attitude toward losses comes from a healthy spirituality. And a healthy spirituality finds God in all things. Sister Phyllis Hughes shares with us how she has been led to find God in all things:

> In the course of a telephone conversation one evening, Jim asked me the following question: "How do you find God in all things?" My immediate response… is this: "I find God in the beauty and goodness of the people who are in my life, in the freshness and newness of nature especially at the moment when Spring with all its wonderment and new life surrounds us."
>
> God is at the centre of my being, of my reason for living and he continually surrounds me in my everyday life, in people and situations I encounter.
>
> My answer to the question was immediate and sincere, but while reflecting on this question since that evening, I realise that, yes, I do find God in the vastness of the sea, the wonder in a child's eyes, in the love of my family, friends and members of my community.

---

15 Carol Soussey, *The Art of Growing Old* (Minneapolis: Augsburg Fortress Publications, 1998), 52.
16 As above.

I find God in the stillness of my prayer. Christ comes alive in the listening to and the praying of the Gospels, through the celebration, the sharing and the living out of the Eucharist and reconciliation. I am aware of my need of the Spirit and the strength which she gives. God is very close too when I listen to others and pray with them in their struggles and joys. The trust given to me and the trust that I give to others is for me a true discovery of God in my life and in all life.

Being an optimist by nature, it has always been relatively easy for me to find God in beauty, stillness, love and wonder. My journey through the latter years of my life has really brought me to find God in pain and suffering.

I have had to struggle to find him in the pain and questioning of the sudden death of my younger brother. There has been a struggle too because of events and situations surrounding my apostolic mission in life. Pain, confusion and even questioning God himself have brought me to a deeper and perhaps a more real relationship with him.

Pain and suffering were no strangers to me in the earlier years of my life, but somehow during the stage of mid-life I have been led to discover and embrace God through the reality of the Paschal Mystery (death and resurrection of Jesus), in my own brokenness and fragility, in my dying and my rising.

In the past few years of my life I have struggled with poor health. Optimists usually enjoy life to the full, and I am no exception! To experience physical weakness, to arrive at acknowledging my dependency on others, having to admit to being unreliable have brought me to an awareness of my complete and utter dependence on God.

It has been and continues to be a painful journey but I am deeply convinced of the personal love that God has for me and of my love for him. Yes, I know that God is in the joys and dreams, the sorrows and brokenness of my life. I can identify more and more with the words of St Paul: "When I am weak, then I am strong."

Sister Phyllis clearly identifies her own experience of life as the major source of God's presence. We can highlight where she finds God:

- in beauty and goodness
- at the centre of her being
- in listening to and praying the Gospels
- in listening to others
- in pain, confusion and questioning
- in brokenness and fragility
- in the experience of physical weakness and dependency.

As the Vatican Council said: "The joy and hope, the grief and anguish of the men of our time, especially of those who are poor or afflicted in any way, are the joy and hope, the grief and anguish of the followers of Christ as well."[17] God does not anaesthetise us against pain; he is not a panacea for all our woes. Sister Phyllis shares, from her own personal experience, the view of philosopher John Macmurray:

> The maxim of illusory religion runs: "Fear not; trust in God and he will see that none of the things you fear will happen to you"; that of real religion, on the contrary, is: "Fear not; the things that you are afraid of are quite likely to happen to you, but they are nothing to be afraid of."[18]

God is present with us in all our struggles, sustaining, encouraging and enabling us to face each new day with confidence, despite its troubles. He never said that we would not have troubles, but he did promise to be with us in them. Indeed, as St Paul discovered, because God helps us in our troubles we are able to help others in their troubles:

17 *Gaudium et Spes*, 1.
18 Cited by William A. Barry, *Paying Attention to God* (Notre Dame: Ave Maria Press, 1990), 29.

Blessed be the God and Father of our Lord Jesus Christ, a gentle Father and the God of all consolation, who comforts us in all our sorrows, so that we can offer others, in their sorrows, the consolation that we have received from God ourselves (2 Corinthians 1:3-4).

Contemplating the cross is the best preparation for finding God in all things. God was so present in the crucifixion that it was he himself who died on the cross. Pain, suffering, failure and sickness, even death itself are not closed to God's redeeming presence. God's redeeming presence in Jesus on the cross and in the tomb was the guarantee of the transformation of the resurrection. In the same way God's redeeming presence in all the circumstances of our lives, good or bad, guarantees our final victory in our resurrection from the dead.

We can celebrate the sacrament of the present moment using very simple, ordinary means. St Alphonsus kept a clock on his table which chimed every fifteen minutes. Whenever it did so, Alphonsus opened himself more consciously to the presence of God and lived that moment more intensely aware that God was with him. His example became a great help to me one year. I was a student in our international house in Rome. Just outside my door there was a phone, which rang very frequently, and I was expected to answer it and then find the student to take his phone call. For the first day or two I didn't mind, but I quickly began to resent it. I resented being disturbed at my studies or while at rest. My resentment was turning into anger and unwillingness. Then I got the grace to remember St Alphonsus' clock. The phone could be my spiritual "alarm clock". I said to myself each time that wretched phone rings I will take it as a call from God to become aware of his presence. From then on the ring of the phone woke up my slumbering spirit. As I walked to answer the phone I was able to become aware of God's presence with me. In fact, that phone became the occasion of my best prayer during that year. Every time it rang outside my door I was able to "raise my mind and heart to God". For me God was on the line.

If we practise the presence of God, if we celebrate the sacrament of the present moment in the ordinary situations of daily life, we are training our minds and hearts to find God even in the bad and tragic things. I have always been deeply moved when I have heard old people in Ireland say, in the midst of great suffering or tragedy, "It could be worse, thank God." It is the "thank God" within that response which is so faith-filled and even astonishing. St Patrick tells us that: "God taught me to praise him equally in times of adversity and in times of prosperity." Patrick too would have been saying in the bad times, "It could be worse, thank God". St Patrick was a great contemplative in action.

Practising the presence of God forms within us the contemplative outlook on life. This outlook keeps us trusting and calm, even when things are going wrong. This contemplative outlook enables us to live in the present moment. It is in the present moment that God wishes to hallow his name in our lives. When we pray, "hallowed be thy name", we are praying for the grace to find God in all things and to celebrate the sacrament of the present moment. In all situations we pray with confidence, "hallowed be thy name".

Personal spiritual exercise

- Centre yourself, using the techniques we learned in week one.
- Bring yourself to bodily stillness and calm.
- Now ask yourself: Do I want to live in the present, or do I prefer to escape into the past, or live anxiously in the future? Do I want to encounter God in this present moment?
- Now be still.
- Now focus again on your breathing.
- And bring yourself gently back to the world.